FOR CONSERVATIVES ONLY

A study of Conservative leadership
from Churchill to Heath

By the same author:
RETURN FROM UTOPIA

to
P. V. E–E

FOR CONSERVATIVES ONLY

Lord Coleraine

TOM STACEY LTD

Tom Stacey, Ltd., 11a Stratford Road,
London, W.8., England.

First published 1970

Copyright © Lord Coleraine

SBN 85468 006 3

*Printed in Great Britain by
Richard Clay (The Chaucer Press), Ltd.,
Bungay, Suffolk.*

CONTENTS

PREFACE

There is little that I can usefully add to the essay which follows, except, perhaps, to say that it is not intended as an election programme and that its purpose is not to make converts. I wrote it in order to clear my own mind about the relevance of Conservatism in a period of violent change; and if it should help other Conservatives to clear theirs, too, I shall be well content, even if it does not lead them to the same conclusions.

I would like, however, to thank those to whom I feel that I owe a special debt of gratitude. Sir Herbert Butterfield's *Christianity and History* made a deep impression on me when I first read it twenty years ago, and has much influenced my thought ever since. I am grateful to him for permission to quote from it. I am grateful, too, to Sir Isaiah Berlin for allowing me to call in aid *Four Essays on Liberty* and I must thank the Fabian Society for permitting me to quote freely from Mr. R. H. S. Crossman's *Paying for the Social Services*.

To Mrs. Diana Spearman, with whom I have discussed almost every line that I have written, and who, in a very real sense (if she will allow the aspersion), is co-author, I am deeply grateful. And I must thank those also who have been kind enough to read the manuscript, Lord Salisbury, Sir Arthur Bryant, Mr. Robert Blake, Sir Paul Grey, Sir Derrick Gunston, Mr. John Wood and

Mr. R. E. Artus in particular. None of these is responsible for what I say, and none agrees with all of it, but I am most grateful to them for their criticisms and suggestions.

Finally, I must thank most warmly my secretary, Mrs. Deverell, whose patience and continuing interest in my essay as it proceeded were alike remarkable.

CHAPTER I

CONSERVATISM IN AN AGE OF
REVOLUTION

1

We have lived, in the twentieth century, through an upheaval which, for its scale and intensity, is without parallel in the recorded history of man. Political and economic systems, faith and morals, our conceptions of time and space, everything is in a state of flux. At such a time, it is natural to ask, what place can there be for Conservatism or a Conservative party? When the human situation is being so radically transformed, and when it is clearly necessary for man-made institutions, and the society which they serve, to adapt themselves as rapidly as may be to conditions that are utterly new, what can be the relevance of a political philosophy of which the essence is reverence for the past, and which bases itself upon the lessons of experience rather than the hopes or necessities of the future? What relevance can it have, in particular, for a country like Britain which, with the rest of the world but under a compulsion even more imperative, is seeking to adjust itself to a revolution of unprecedented violence; and which, at the same time, has to take account of its own changed position in a changed world?

The answers one gives to questions like these cannot be the result of simple calculation and the balancing of advantages against disadvantages. They depend far more on one's view of politics and the purposes of society, and especially on one's view of man's nature and his place in the scheme of things. But the quick answer, the easy answer and the answer that is generally given, even by the leaders of the Conservative party itself, is that Conservatism no longer has any meaning as a political philosophy, and that a Conservative party, if it is to be an effective political force, must turn its back on the past and itself become a party of progress, differing from its opponents not in its outlook or in the ends which it serves, but only in the means which it uses to realise them.

But it is just when there is general agreement on wide-ranging issues of this kind that one should be most wary. When all are of one mind, and when no hypothesis is submitted to a critical judgement, the chances of error are very great, all the greater because no one can imagine the possibility of error. Looking at the world about us, and reflecting on the times through which we have lived, can we be sure that the past has nothing to teach us? We have effectively freed ourselves from the bonds of tradition. Have we been vindicated by the event? Or must we recognise in our day a lamentable disintegration in the fabric of western society, and a fall in the standards of human behaviour, which would have been inconceivable in, say, the summer of 1914—or, for the matter of that, in the summer of 1814? When we begin to ask ourselves questions of this kind it becomes possible, at least, to believe that we may have been too hasty in our rejection of the past, and that it is precisely in times like these, when old certainties are dissolved and old landmarks obliterated, that we most need its lessons.

The world which came to an end in 1914 was disfigured, no doubt, by poverty and suffering, and there were pressures building up which must explode if they were not relieved. But even allowing for the fact that the security of the pre-1914 world was largely an illusion, and that to those who were living then, and responsible for the conduct of affairs, the future was filled with foreboding; even accepting that security and stability were the last blessings that our fathers conceived themselves to be enjoying (for they could already feel the tremors of the earth beneath their feet); allowing for all this, there was still in that world a sense of order and reason altogether missing from our own. A distinguished and experienced American statesman has written of the years before 1914:

'The world was stable and predictable. During the hundred years after Waterloo Englishmen and Americans believed themselves moving on the great current of Progress to the reign of universal peace and universal law. . . . For a hundred years international war had been held to a minimum; economic and technical progress in the century then just ending had exceeded that of the whole prior history of man; and the existence of one world had been achieved as never before or since. People, goods and ideas moved about with an unequalled freedom, and the lives of people everywhere were moulded by a gigantic world-wide scheme.'*

* Dean Acheson, *Fifty Years After*, Yale Review, Autumn 1961.

13

The Concert of Europe and the Monroe Doctrine, if they did not guarantee order, ensured, at least, that disorder was kept within bounds, for there was no one whose interest it was to promote disorder. Prudence and common sense, untainted by idealism or the urge to set the world to rights, were enough to maintain a general equilibrium. Precarious and unreal as its unity proved in the event to be, the world before 1914 was like a planetary system, ordered, regular and predictable, by comparison with our own.

There is no need to speculate here on the causes of its collapse—from Sedan and Agadir, through the Somme and Verdun and Versailles, to the Rhineland, Munich, Yalta and beyond. Many people, and most young people, believe that the sickness from which the world is suffering today is due to the inflexible conservatism of those who have been in control, their aversion to any kind of innovation and their utter inability to adapt themselves to changing conditions. But to suppose this is to stand history on its head. Whether one considers the violent men who engineered disaster, or the honourably fatuous who strove to avert it, it was not the reactionaries who were in the saddle: it was the men of vision.

It could be said of Louis Napoleon without too much injustice that he, more than any man, was the one who upset the apple-cart, for he cleared the road for Bismarck. But he was no conservative: egotist, dreamer and incompetent dictator, he was the very model of a progressive, ready to stir up trouble wherever he could find it, if only it could be supposed to serve the ends of progress. And if Bismarck was a Junker and a Conservative, his conservatism was of a very special kind which up-

14

rooted a thousand years of German history to make the German empire. Hitler and Mussolini were revolutionaries. Woodrow Wilson and Franklin Roosevelt were the most powerful men in the world during the most critical years of the century. The one fastened on Europe the outdated and dangerously irrelevant principle of 'the self-determination of peoples'. The other, believing that British colonialism was a greater threat to freedom than Russian democracy, made over half of Europe to the Soviets and half the world to anarchy. Both were progressives and liberals. 'It is essential,' says Professor Butterfield, 'not to have faith in human nature. Such faith is a very recent heresy and a very disastrous one.'* One has only to compare the settlements of Vienna and Versailles, or contrast the outlook of Castlereagh and Metternich with that of Lloyd George and Woodrow Wilson, to understand the truth of this bleak aphorism. It is sheer illusion to suppose that western civilisation has gone half way back to barbarism because it was in the control of backward looking men. It was not. They looked forward with hope and unquestioning assurance. That was their trouble—and ours.

2

But history is not the work of statesmen alone. It is made up, even more, of the habits, the impulses and the illusions of ordinary men and women. And when we consider what is happening today over a great part of the world—immaturity, indiscipline and emotional instability in the young; fatalism, uncertainty and lack of con-

* Herbert Butterfield, *Christianity and History* p. 47.

fidence among their elders; the collapse of religious faith and the breakdown of traditional morality; the growing habit of violence with its mounting threat to order and freedom—we cannot easily persuade ourselves that it is due to the crippling influence of tradition. For good or ill, this world of ours is a monument to the idea of progress and the perfectibility of man.

When we look at the world around us, and when we consider the changes that have taken place in it during our lives and which are still taking place, it is easy to feel that human institutions must be changed rapidly, and if necessary violently, to match this new environment. But to believe that change is all, and that it is only necessary to remodel society, as it might be to reconstruct a house, is to forget that society is made up of human beings, not of bricks and mortar, and that we understand but imperfectly the forces which influence it. It is to forget, too, that if human nature is handled too roughly it will find ways of taking its revenge. The problem is not simply to change society and its institutions, but to change them in such a way as to hold in check, not license, man's instinct for aggression, and to support, not weaken, his capacity for development. Even in a changing world, especially in a changing world, conservatism has a contribution to make, and one of great importance: it is to remind us that man is a being supremely valuable in his own right, and that he cannot properly be regarded as a convenient raw material for the social reformer.

Twentieth-century man feels himself, in especial degree, to be at the mercy of his environment, and powerless to control or even influence it. It is this feeling of helplessness, at the very time when he might have

thought himself to be as never before the Lord of Creation, which explains the lack of confidence, not only in
himself but in the meaning and purpose of his life,
which especially distinguishes western man from his
forebears.

And yet this environment, which seems to him at once
hostile and beyond the reach of his influence, is his own
artefact. He is not threatened by some monstrous asser-
tion of the powers of nature external to himself: it
might be better for him if he were, for then, at least, he
could fight back. The threat comes from his own self-
will. Before he can master his environment he must
master himself. It is here that tradition, with its long
reach back to the accumulated experience of mankind,
can help him when nothing else can. It is precisely because tradition is a protection against the weaknesses and
excesses of human nature—as hope can never be—that
Conservatives value it, not because it represents for them
a harking back to vanished glories, or a putting back of
the clock. The past sixty years, if they have nothing else
to teach us, show how much we need that protection and
how, without it, there is no limit to human wickedness
and folly, or to the degradation to which they lead.

Nor can we persuade ourselves that the evils which
have disgraced our day are due to the especial wickedness of particular peoples.

'Some of us have become so accustomed to a humane
form of society, which cushions the conflicts between
men and mitigates the self-aggression, that we imagine
its virtues to spring straight out of nature with no
more cultivation than the wild flowers on the bank of

a stream. We almost come to think of human beings as creatures naturally civilised, so that when we are confronted with a spectacle of barbarous conduct on a wide scale we are content to stop at the first stage of the argument and say that here are millions of men stupendously wicked, worse than human nature itself. We do not go far enough in considering what is implied in such a general lapse into barbarism, or reflect how precarious our civilised existence will always be, if, almost in absence of mind, we allow certain of the guards to be taken off. The virtues of western society in modern times were in reality the product of much education, tradition and discipline; they needed centuries of patient cultivation. Even without great criminality in anybody—merely by forgetting certain safeguards—we could lose the tolerance and urbanities, the respect for human life and human personality, which are in reality the late blossoms of a highly developed civilisation.'*

Things have happened as they did happen because, one by one, the restraints were removed which tradition imposes on human behaviour: they will always happen when these restraints are removed.

The danger in which we stand comes not so much from our inability to adapt ourselves to rapid change as from our incapacity, in the face of change so rapid, to uphold the standards of conduct which experience has shown to be necessary for the well-being of man in society. So far from a conservative attitude of mind being an anomaly in a revolutionary age, it is perhaps the con-

* Herbert Butterfield, op. cit., p. 31.

dition of survival. Or do we sincerely believe that the modern world represents such an advance on everything that has gone before that there is nothing to be learned from the past?

3

Conservatives have always shown an aversion to systematic thought, mistrusting dogma and priding themselves on their empiricism. It has been said of Lord Salisbury, the Prime Minister—himself, perhaps, the archetype of the conservative mind—that 'the greater number of the principles by which he was guided were essentially utilitarian in character and founded on what may be called the higher expediency. There were but a few of them for which he would have admitted any independent or permanent existence apart from the circumstances in which they operated.'* And in general, certainly, Conservatives are more concerned with what works in a given situation than with its conformity with any preconceived theory of politics. It is, indeed, just this predisposition for the practical against the theoretical which chiefly distinguishes the conservative from the progressive mind.

It must be conceded, too, that Peel, even more than Salisbury, was guided by principles 'which were essentially utilitarian in character'. He was pre-eminently the 'practical man' without the least trace of philosophic insight.

* *Biographical Studies of the Life and Political Character of Robert, third Marquis of Salisbury,* by Lady Gwendolen Cecil, p. 14.

'As long as Ireland could be governed without grant-
ing Emancipation, he resisted it. As long as he could
work the fiscal administration of the country without
repealing the Corn Laws, he defended them. But the
conversion to which no abstract argument could lead
him was at once asserted by the logic of fact. An im-
pending civil war in Ireland, an actual famine there,
did what no reflections on religious liberty or free
trade would ever have done.'*

And Disraeli prided himself, rather than otherwise, on
being a man of worldly commonsense, uninhibited by
the lofty preconceptions of his great rival.

It would be a mistake, however, to push this argument
too far. It is true that conservatism is an attitude of
mind, not a corpus of doctrine or a carefully worked out
system of political theory. But conservative pragmatism,
even when it seems to be second nature, is not simply
instinctive. It is based on a certain reading of history, a
certain interpretation of experience. Even the most
hidebound of Conservatives is more rational and less
intuitive in his political attitudes than he, or anyone
else, supposes, and Conservatism is grounded in a system
of thought as respectable as any and, more than most,
buttressed by observation and experience.

Any political association which exists to further by
parliamentary action the ends which its members combine to promote, must have a coherent and generally
consistent body of principle on which to base itself.
Without this, there is nothing except self-interest to hold
party members together, and nothing to breed the kind

* Lord Hugh Cecil, *Conservatism*, p. 68.

of conviction which attracts support and generates action. This is not to say that a political party must be a close-knit band of zealots, burning with passion and hamstrung by dogma. It does imply, however, some kind of intellectual and philosophic background to which policy can be referred, and which can be communicated, in however simplified a form, to a mass electorate, not so much to attract it as in some sense to reflect it and engage its loyalty.

It implies, also, the existence in the central direction of the party of a hard core of conviction to ensure, as far as it is possible to ensure it, that the permanent ends to be served by the party are not sacrificed to the exigencies of the moment. A party leader cannot be blamed if the pressure of events forces him to turn aside from some cherished goal, but he is foolish indeed if he consistently pursues a course which is manifestly against the convictions of his followers, convictions of which he is the high priest and the guardian. For the leader owes a loyalty to his followers as real as any that is due from them to him, and when he neglects it not only is he betraying a trust: he is cutting at the roots of his own power.

For the Conservative, this background of essential conviction comes from the fusion of two great political traditions, the Tory and the Whig. To the one, the Conservative owes his understanding of the dark and frightening propensities in human nature which have revealed themselves with renewed starkness in our own day, and of the importance of the institutions which keep these in check. From the other, he draws his belief in freedom and his respect for the individual, not as a social unit but as the uniquely valuable being whose interests society exists to serve. The two sets of principles—the importance of society as a check upon man's folly and wickedness, and respect for the individual as a check upon the pretensions of society—are complementary. Each holds the other in bounds. But it was not always so. From the Revolution of 1688, which marked the beginnings of the party system as we know it, until the end of the eighteenth century and later, these principles were opposed. It was the French Revolution which drew them together. On the one side, the Whig saw what happened when Freedom and the Enlightenment were given their head without restraint. The Tory, for his part, was made aware of the evils which followed from the total suppression of freedom and from the rigidities of a caste system. The two philosophies, once opposed, were fused by the genius of Burke, no Tory, but the first, as he remains the greatest, of Conservatives.

Conservatives are often described as 'the stupid party' because the Conservative is guided by instinct as much as by reason. And Burke himself, even if his genius is recognised, is thought of as obscurantist and irrational. 'We are afraid,' he says, 'to put man to live and trade each on his own private stock of reason; because we suspect that this stock in each man is small and that the individuals would do better to avail themselves of the general bank and capital of the ages and of the nations.'

It is sometimes believed that Burke's view that man inherits the experience and the memories of his ancestors as he inherits the colour of their hair or their eyes, is no more than an intellectual conceit, a fanciful metaphor, an illusion. But yesterday's certainties are eroded

22

by the new knowledge of today, and if there is one thing more important than any other that we suppose ourselves to have learned in the last half century, it is that the part of man's mind of which he is conscious is not the only part and that it is probably the least important part.

'In studying reactions to early traumata, we often find to our confusion that they do not keep strictly to what the individual himself has experienced, but deviate from this in a way that would accord much better with their reactions to genetic events, and in general can be explained only through the influence of such. . . . If the so-called instincts of animals—which from the very beginning allow them to behave in their new conditions of living, as if they were old and well-established ones—if this instinctual life of animals permits of any explanation at all, it can only be this, that they carry over into their new existence the experience of their kind, that is to say that they have preserved in their minds memories of what their ancestors experienced. In the human animal things should not be fundamentally different.'*

In spite of the obscurity of his language, it is evident that Freud is on Burke's side, that he, too, belongs to the stupid party. Not only is Burke the greatest of Conservatives: he is the most modern, too.

Lord Morley said that for Burke the cardinal truth for man was 'that if you encourage every individual to let the imagination loose upon all subjects, without any restraint from a sense of his own weakness, and his subor-

* Sigmund Freud, *Moses and Monotheism.*

dinate role in the long scheme of things, then there is nothing of all that the opinion of ages has agreed to regard as excellent and venerable, which would not be exposed to destruction at the hand of rationalistic criticism'.* What was true of Burke's day is true of ours. And if we have witnessed horrors which would have appalled Robespierre or Marat if they could have conceived of them, there is similarity enough between the Terror and the Concentration Camp, the guillotine and the gas-chamber, the storming of the Bastille and student rioting at the Sorbonne or Berkeley University or the London School of Economics, to point Burke's moral for us: man, when he relies on his own unaided judgement, without the restraint of tradition and the accumulated experience of the past, is less attractive than the other carnivores, and no more to be trusted than they.

It is this awareness of man's weakness and folly, not class interest or any doctrinaire conception of how the state should be organised, that leads the Conservative to distrust sudden and drastic change, and all policies which depend upon it. He recognises that, once the structure of society has been weakened beyond a certain point, there is no crime too horrifying for human beings, even highly cultivated and intelligent human beings, to commit, Indeed, it is the danger of the total breakdown of civilisation which induces him to tolerate inefficiencies, and even injustices, rather than put social stability at risk.

Of course this attitude of mind, like all political attitudes, can be carried too far, but there are more solid grounds for it than many people, even many Conserv-

* Quoted by Morley, *Burke* (English Men of Letters), p. 15.

atives, will admit. It is natural enough, when civilisation is apparently securely founded, to mock the Conservative tradition. It is odd that it should be so much out of favour in our own day when the lie, mass murder, torture and the systematic destruction of the human personality have served over a great part of the world as the ordinary currency of politics, and when even in our own relatively mature society violence and irrationality are increasingly in evidence.

Because of the unpalatable lessons which experience, his own and that of history, has taught him, the Conservative can never be a mere reactionary. He is chary of experimentation just because he realises that institutions and traditions, once destroyed or qualified, cannot be put back as they were, and that the attempt to do so may let loose forces as dangerous, destructive and uncontrollable as revolution itself.

Still less do Conservatives have sympathy with that twentieth-century mixture of reaction and revolution which is called Fascism. Indeed it is impossible for anyone who does not have unqualified faith in the natural goodness of man to contemplate with an easy mind the thought of absolute power in the hands of any individual, however enlightened, or any group of individuals. History is one long illustration of the dangers of centralised autocracy, and recent developments in psychology, medicine and genetics have enormously multiplied these dangers. Fascists, if no one else, understood quite clearly that Conservatives could never be their allies, and that the destruction of all those classes and interests supposed to be naturally conservative, was a prerequisite of the Fascist revolution.

25

'For fifty years generals, diplomats and bureaucrats have been taken from the upper classes and from a limited number of families of wealth and position. It is time to put an end to all this, if we want to infuse new energy and new blood into the nation.'*

It is not Mr. Harold Wilson or Mr. Edward Short who speaks. It is Benito Mussolini.

It is one of the curiosities of modern history, and a remarkable endorsement of the effectiveness of the propaganda of the Left, that Fascism, a revolutionary movement identified, as its name indicates, with the subordination of the individual to the state, should be equated in the popular mind with conservative reaction. It is worth remembering, too, that the term 'Nazi' is an abbreviation for National Socialism, and that Hitler's government was indeed a socialist government, even if its socialism was more extreme, and in some respects more efficient, than anything we have known here.

4

The Conservative's respect for experience is not just a kind of superstition. The fact that a tradition cannot be explained does not mean that it is unreasonable. It may only mean that we have forgotten the reason.

'Turkish farmers leave their stones on the cultivated fields. When asked why, they say that it is the way it has always been done and that it is better that way. In point of fact it is. When United Nations agronomists,

* Quoted by Diana Spearman, *Modern Dictatorship*, p. 144.

after considerable exhortation, persuaded some young Turks to remove the stones from the fields, their crops suffered. Apparently the stones help condense and contain the dew in an arid climate, but this was unknown. It may have been known to the originators of the custom, for there is evidence that it was known in biblical times. This apparent fact had been forgotten while the practice persisted.'*

A tradition, it is true, may outlive its usefulness, but it may still be imprudent to discard it. Tradition is an integral part of the framework of society, and if for uncounted time the life of a people has been regulated by traditional forms of behaviour, or traditional relationships, to cut these off at a stroke only because they are no longer seen to be relevant, may be to disturb the stability of society itself.†

The English class system, for instance, has no very obvious justification today, and the nexus of privilege and responsibility which it once reflected has been much weakened, if it has not disappeared. And yet the insis-

---

* 'Is there Reason in Tradition?' Samuel Coleman, *Politics and Experience: Essays presented to Michael Oakeshott*, Cambridge University Press.

† 'We should be anxious, terrified and frustrated, and we could not live in a social world, did it not contain a considerable amount of order, a great number of regularities to which we can adjust ourselves. The mere existence of these regularities is perhaps more important than their peculiar merits or demerits. They are needed as regularities and are therefore handed on as traditions, whether they are not in other respects rational or necessary or good or beautiful or what you will. There is need for tradition in social life.'

R. Park and E. W. Burgess, *Introduction to the Science of Sociology*, quoted by Coleman, op. cit.

tence of the progressive upon the unqualified evil of what has come to be known, in the prevailing cant, as 'social divisiveness', may be exaggerated. It is a paradox certainly, but it may be more than a coincidence, that the western society which, more than any other, has been distinguished by its homogenity and cohesiveness has also been that in which the class structure has been the most elaborate and the most clearly marked.

It is perhaps too readily assumed that if only class distinctions are obliterated, there will be unity in a divided nation and, in consequence, a release of new and vital energy. Indeed, to hear some people talk one might suppose that all our ills, social, moral and economic, derive from our class structure. But the class system in this country has never been a caste system. It has always been possible, indeed easy, to pass from one class to another—either upwards or downwards—so that the class structure has been nothing like as rigid as many people suppose. And although the Englishman is class-conscious by comparison, say, with the American, he has not usually been resentful of class or felt a sense of inferiority on account of it. Equality has never appealed to him as an ideal, as freedom or fairness appeal to him. It might almost be said of him that he does more than accept distinctions of class and rank; and that he welcomes them because they assure him of a stable place in a stable society. There is a very real sense in which the class structure, as it has been developed and modified through centuries of English history, is a guarantee of liberty.

For when all is said, a man must regulate his relationships with his fellows somehow, or he is adrift and alone in an unfriendly universe. And it may be that some of the unease, frustration and unhappiness which, to the shocked surprise of the Christian humanist, are the accompaniment of rapidly rising material standards, is due to the too sudden dissolution of the system of social relationships which has persisted in England from time immemorial, and for which no effective substitute has been devised. All that we are doing, perhaps, by our persistent hankering after equality, is replacing a society in which each man has a responsibility towards his neighbour, and a respect for him, by a kind of flux, the chance coming together and drifting apart of indifferent atoms. We have substituted for a class struggle which, in England, has been tempered by common loyalties and mutual respect, a free-for-all of bitterly contesting groups—carpenters, welders, brick-layers, stockbrokers, teachers, airline pilots, doctors, what you will—each intent on grasping from the common stock the greatest share of what is to be had.

5

The Conservative is sceptical, too, of grand designs for the elevation of mankind. It is possible to believe that nuclear war will mean the final collapse of western civilisation, without accepting as a necessary corollary that the United Nations, an organisation disproportionately influenced by that part of the human race most lacking in political experience and most backward in the development of political, social and juridical institutions, is capable of averting such a disaster. Again, it is possible to believe, with Edith Cavell, that 'patriotism is not enough' without concluding that it is nothing, and that the feeling which a man has for that complex of memories, pictorial images, relationships, affections, traditions and prejudices which he knows as his country, can be transferred at will to some abstraction called World Government or United Europe.

It is curious how in these days the politician, and especially the progressive politician, never refers to his country but always to 'the nation': the nation demands this, or the nation will not tolerate that. And this is not a distinction without a difference, for it expresses the whole difference between patriotism and nationalism. 'The nation' connotes a group of people living in the present, looking neither to the past nor to the future, concerned only with immediate ends, and, in Burke's words, themselves no better than the flies of summer. The signal which flew from the masthead of Victory at Trafalgar was 'England expects . . .', not 'the Nation expects' or 'the Community expects . . .'. It was the idea of England that in the end defeated Napoleon, an idea linking one generation with another, through the whole continuum of time. The idea of his country is a reality to an Englishman, and to deprive him of it, or to persuade him that it is something shameful, is as sensible as to force the idea of patriotism on the Central African, or equate nationalism with tribalism and political freedom with majority rule.

To the left-wing intellectual, of course, the idea of patriotism is essentially a class conception, and a middle-class, public school conception at that, without roots in human nature or human history. But it is worth remembering that Trafalgar ante-dates the headmastership of

Dr. Arnold by several years, and that Shakespeare, Ovid and Thucydides ante-date it by even more. The problem today is how to build a wider loyalty upon the foundation of patriotism, not how to destroy patriotism. It is not possible to move from the idea of England to the idea, say, of a United States of Europe by any purely intellectual decision. It is certain that new political and social relationships must evolve if this shrunken world is to survive, but they must come from the realities of experience and from men's hearts. Lloyd George used to say that you cannot take two steps across an abyss. As an expression of the progressive outlook this could hardly be bettered, but the fact remains that if the abyss is too broad for leaping, it is still necessary to find a way round it or build a bridge across it. There are problems which cannot be solved by rhetoric.

6

This is not to say that Britain must not enter the Common Market, only that the argument ought not to be based on denunciations of the wickedness of patriotism or upon crude calculations of profit or loss. When, for example, the B.B.C. moves to ban the singing at Promenade concerts of 'Land of Hope and Glory' or 'Rule Britannia', because such expressions of nationalistic fervour are thought to be offensive to visitors from abroad, it is being ridiculous, no doubt, but it is disregarding human nature and history alike. It is possible, even when France is a member of the Common Market, for a Frenchman to sing the 'Marseillaise' without impropriety, and a Yorkshireman can sing 'On Ilkley Moor bar t'at' and still send his representatives to Westminster. Life in France and Yorkshire alike would be the poorer if the pedantry of some youthful intellectual in the broadcasting service were allowed to interfere with the expression of such emotions, and a United Europe, so conceived, would be still-born.

For the Treaty of Rome will only become a reality if it is founded securely in the European tradition, that is to say if it takes full account of the fact that there are differences between Frenchmen, Englishmen and Germans just as there are differences between cockneys, Yorkshiremen and Cornishmen. To try to suppress these distinctions, instead of finding ways in which they can express themselves naturally and harmlessly, is not to create a new European society. It is to build a mechanistic model, something to be galvanised into a sort of activity, no doubt, by the appropriate stimulus, but never to have a life of its own.

A man cannot express himself fully, it is true, except as a member of a community. He has a natural loyalty to his family, which he can extend without undue strain to his village or his county or his city, and which he can extend again to his country. Within these loyalties, and because of them, his personality expands and develops. But if you break down these limited loyalties in order to substitute for them a wider loyalty—if you tell a man that his duty is not to his family but to the community, and not to his country but to the world of mankind—you are only creating a vacuum. A man cannot change his loyalties to order, or move from a local community which he knows to an international community which is foreign to him, by any act of will.

These facts constitute a very real dilemma when we consider the world of the twentieth and the twenty-first centuries. On the one hand, it has grown so small that the nation state is an anachronism, at best irrelevant, at worst highly dangerous. On the other, if you sweep away the nation state which until now has been a focus of loyalty, there is no kind of guarantee that the European community which you substitute for it will attract the same loyalty. Everything that we know of the nature of man in society suggests that it will not.

There is only one possibility of escape from this dilemma. It is to ensure that the transition from the one organisation to the other is gradual, and that it is based on the continuance of existing loyalties and not, as so many supporters of the idea of a United Europe seem to demand, on their destruction.

Nor, ultimately, will Britain's entry into Europe, or Europe's future, depend on the price of butter and eggs. Of course a United Europe, like any other social organisation, must have an economic base, what is called, in modern parlance, an infrastructure, but that is not what binds society together. In the end it is something deeply rooted in human nature, the instinct of self-preservation, for instance, which changes a Heptarchy into a kingdom or a tribal society into a nation.

To look across the Atlantic, and to see that great republic, for so long the repository of human hopes, grappling desperately with problems which seem almost insoluble, and which will certainly preoccupy it for many years to come; to watch on the television screen an anniversary parade in the Red Square in Moscow; to reflect not only on the 'hardware' to be seen, the ballistic missiles, the artillery and the armour, but also on the superb precision of the troops with all their pride and self-confidence; to see all this is to feel, perhaps, that only a Europe united in defence (something very different from a European alliance) can save itself or preserve our own island security.

The argument for a United Europe used to be based on the hypothesis that world wars had a habit of starting in Europe, and that a third world war could be avoided if the infected area could be sterilised. But the third world war may start anywhere in the world, and Europe has lost even that doubtful distinction which it once enjoyed as a focus of infection. For Europe, the cradle of western civilisation, has the status today of an outlying province of Rome, a Dacia or a Gaul, when it is set beside the Soviet Union or the United States (and soon, no doubt, Communist China). If we think European culture worth preserving perhaps we should exert ourselves to preserve it, by giving Western Europe a life of its own.

CHAPTER II

THE IDEA OF A SPONTANEOUS ORDER

1

It is his feeling for the fragility of civilisation which makes the Conservative distrustful of sudden change, and certainly a Conservative party which makes an idol of modernisation, which sees itself as dragging Britain, an unruly child, kicking and screaming into the twentieth century, is abrogating its most important function: that is, to test the new idea against experience.

But it is the essence of the Conservative approach to the problems of man in society that society is a living organism which, like any other, like man himself, has its being in three dimensions—the past, the present and the future. It follows from this that the capacity to change and to adapt itself is the condition of its survival. The fact that society is a living, sentient thing, not a mechanical contrivance, means, however, that it can be harmed, perhaps irremediably, by rash and ill-considered innovations. You may tamper with a machine, and if you damage one of its parts you can order another from a drawing. But there is no blueprint for society and the phrase 'social engineering', so much beloved of the progressive politician, is as misleading as it is dangerous.

Burke draws a distinction, which is still, even in the twentieth century, cardinal for Conservative thought, between change and reform. Reform is directed to remedying a specific evil, and even if it turns out in the event to have been misdirected, the harm that is done is limited to the limb or the organ, so to say, which is infected. Change, on the other hand, is a process which affects the whole chemistry of the body, and it is impossible in practice to limit or circumscribe its effects. As Burke insists, it is not enough to identify a social evil: the problem is how to remedy it without creating new evils, greater or more widespread than the old.

Because wholesale innovation has results which cannot be foreseen and guarded against, and because even reform, in the Burkeian use of the word, can bring in its train consequences which are unexpected,* it would be very much better if the social system had enough flexibility in itself, and enough sensitivity, to respond to the need for change without deliberate intervention from outside. If this degree of flexibility exists change, because it is continuous, need never be violent. If it exists, it is unnecessary to wait until an evil becomes intolerable before it is remedied, for the necessary adjustments will have been made at an earlier stage. It is at this point that the Tory tradition of rational order meets and fuses with the Whig tradition of rational freedom to produce a society that is ordered, free and reasonable.

It is necessary here to clear away certain misconceptions. It is increasingly assumed, in Conservative as in other circles, that personal liberty is in some way antisocial. It may be true that other things, security for instance, are more highly valued in Britain today than

* See Karl Popper, *The Open Society and its Enemies* and *Conjectures and Refutation*.

36

freedom. It would seem, indeed, that to many intellectuals the only freedom which is prized is sexual freedom. But no doubt there exists in the minds of many otherwise sensible people the feeling, muddled and confused though it is, that there is something selfish and immoral about the Whig conception of personal liberty, that it is destructive of the social conscience and in some way opposed to the interests of the community as a whole. This is a feeling which is not confined to liberals and socialists. It exists among Conservatives, subjected without respite to the propaganda of the progressive intellectual, and the victims, too, of their own misreading of history. For most Conservatives believe, on no other evidence than that Lord Shaftesbury was a Conservative and that the young Disraeli talked a lot about 'the condition of the people', that in the nineteenth century all Conservatives were in favour of social reform and all Liberals opposed to it. Of course this is a caricature of nineteenth-century politics, as much of a caricature as the idea that the philosophy of *laissez-faire* meant that the weakest should go to the wall or that the devil should take the hindmost.

For the antithesis between the freedom of the individual to pursue his own ends, and the well-being of society in general, is a false one. Personal freedom is as necessary for society as for the individuals who comprise it. It is necessary because it allows for the development of a spontaneous order in economic and social life which, without it, would require deliberate organisation of a kind and on a scale of which the human mind has thus far shown itself to be quite incapable. The true antithesis is not between individual freedom and the needs

37

of society, but between an order which is spontaneous and self-regulating, and one which is imposed.*

2

The idea of a spontaneous order, once taken for granted, is not acceptable in these days. Although we are surrounded by evidence to the contrary—language, for example, which grows and changes through the unco-ordinated activities of innumerable individuals—it is assumed that there cannot be order of any kind unless it has been imposed by some external agency.

Of course there are cases where order has to be imposed: a planned order may be desirable and even necessary when the numbers involved are limited, and the area of uncertainty fairly narrowly circumscribed, or when there is no other way of doing what needs to be done. Tasks directed towards known and limited ends—the manufacture of a range of commodities, the organisation and equipment of an army, space travel or the development of a sewage system—all these must be the subject of direction: they cannot organise themselves. But when the material to be controlled consists of vast numbers of individuals, each with his own problems, his own dreams and his own self-regarding interests, and when, as a consequence, the area of unpredictability is infinite, a planned order must break down. Any plan, even if it is only a plan to catch a train, depends on assumptions about the future, and when these cover the

* For a full discussion of the idea of a spontaneous order, see Hayek, *The Constitution of Liberty*, and Polanyi, *The Logic of Liberty*.

whole range of social and economic activity they cease to have any validity. Analysis gives place to soothsaying, and in this field, at any rate, the prophet is justly without honour, in his own or any other country.

The sheer impossibility of detailed economic planning is now generally recognised, at any rate by Conservatives, but there remains what is called 'indicative' planning. If government cannot organise supply and demand, and if it cannot supervise the minutiae of production and distribution, then surely it must have the duty of identifying economic trends, and of persuading industry to conform to them. Government, after all, commands sources of information and possesses statistical services which private industry cannot match. Does it not follow, then, that it is only through a centralised agency, endowed with the omniscience and the authority of government, that industry can get the basic statistical information from which alone future trends can be predicted, and be induced to act upon it?

But the problem is by no means so simple. Whether it is that the information available to the central agency is already out of date before it can be collected and collated; or whether it never had any more substantial foundation than that provided by a busy factory manager driven frantic by the multiplicity of the forms which he is expected to fill up, and determined only to be rid of them at any cost in terms of accuracy and completeness; or for whatever reason, the efforts of government to plan even indicatively have never been successful except in those fields where, because of the nature of the tasks to be performed, an imposed order is practicable. There is no reason whatever to suppose that

39

government is able to identify economic trends as accurately or as speedily as industry itself. There are several millions of reasons to suggest that it will not. Moreover, the mere appearance of the plan, no matter how its predictions are falsified by the event, distorts the economy because, if decisions are in fact made on the basis of the plan, they are made for reasons which have no validity apart from that which is given them by the plan.*

But a spontaneous order in the economic field does not depend upon the supposed infallibility of a few individuals at the centre, supported and nourished by a mass of information coming in from the periphery with varying degrees of unpunctuality and inaccuracy. It is created and sustained by the self-regarding activities of an almost infinite number of individuals, each of whom is in communication with only a very small number of others. Each one of these, in his turn, is linked to others again. Thus, the needs and ideas of a single person can be communicated through an endless chain to those utterly remote from him, of whose very existence he may be unaware; and everyone in the chain is free to respond to information reaching him, in any way he pleases—or not to respond at all. It is this process, infinitely complex in its operation but infallible in its effects, which causes

---

* 'Think how often in the past ten or fifteen years the assumptions which the planners made were wrong. They were wrong about the capacity of the building industry, wrong about the demand for coal, wrong about the dollar shortage that was to last a generation, wrong about the pattern of our export trade, wrong about steel. On the other hand, when we look at our biggest successes, at the lines and markets on which our export performance and our prosperity depend today, we find them in directions where the planners of ten years ago never looked.' *Freedom and Reality,* by Enoch Powell.

40

packets of tea, for instance, to appear in the grocer's shop in convenient sizes, with blends and flavours suited to the varying tastes of the housewife, and matched to the length of her purse, an operation which is carried out so smoothly that its complexity is not even suspected.

But this kind of intercommunication is by no means confined to specific operations like the production and distribution of a single commodity. It covers the whole field of economic activity. And the same process which creates economic trends, by changing the pattern of supply and demand in oil, or copper, or machine-tools, or tankers, identifies these trends as they appear, more accurately and more swiftly than any centralised planning agency could conceivably do. There is no time-lag of the kind which nullifies the painstaking and earnest research of the planner: there is no fudging of the evidence so that the witness can escape from the box as quickly as may be, and return to his proper job of minding his own business. The process is continuous and the results are immediate, and as accurate as they can be in an uncertain world, with every firm in every industry making its own plans, adjusting them, re-adjusting them and adjusting them again to meet changing conditions. Because of the quasi-infinite number of links in the chain, an order which is spontaneous has a flexibility, a sensitivity and an adaptability that a planned order, monolithic in its structure, can never have.

The reasons for this are easy to grasp. Because a spontaneous order is sustained by a very large number of individuals, modifications and adjustments are being made continuously, not necessarily by everyone within the order, and almost never by everyone at the same time.

But there is continuous adaptation, without violence or sudden disruption. The flexibility of the spontaneous order means, moreover, not only that it responds automatically to changes in its environment, even before these are generally recognised, but also that it is far easier to modify than an order that is imposed. It is easier to supplement the deficiencies of a free economic system through taxation than it is to remedy the defects of, say, a nationalised industry by legislation. A free economic system adjusts itself relatively easily to changes in the law, but the rigidity of an imposed system has the effect that change, even in detail, strains the whole structure. The extreme difficulty of improving a Health Service which is generally thought to be unsatisfactory is a case in point.

There are many who, admitting the greater efficiency of a spontaneous order, hold that the price exacted for it in terms of social cost is too high, and that even gross inefficiency is to be preferred to the suffering which follows the ruthless application of the principles of a free economy. Indeed, any exposition of the theory of a free economy can be counted on to arouse, even in those philosophically opposed to state intervention, dark mutterings about *laissez-faire*, or references to children aroused at three o'clock in the morning to work in textile mills, or to little chimney sweeps with cancer of the skin. But there are still such things as Factory Acts, and it is surely better to control the thoughtlessness, the cruelty or the cupidity of man by legislation than to attempt the impossible task of planning an economy in which there is not even the possibility of abuse.

A spontaneous order, certainly, is careless of the individual units comprising it, nearly as careless as nature herself. It will not protect any particular person, or any particular class, from loss or damage. But that does not mean that there is no protection. Governments, at least in societies as rich as our own, can and should compensate those injured by the impersonality of a spontaneous order, provided always that they do not nullify the benefits to be gained from it. There is no reason, for instance, why the major cost of economic change should fall upon the wage-earner, for there are ways of helping him which will not impair economic efficiency. It is impossible, however, to protect in the same way the business man who goes bankrupt, without damaging the system itself. And yet bankruptcy is a personal misfortune as bitter as, and more final than unemployment. There is more justification than is commonly realised for the rewards that balance the hazards which the entrepreneur must accept.

A spontaneous economic order, then, is more efficient than an imposed order, and it need not be much less humane. It is necessary to stress again, however, that personal liberty is the necessary precondition for it. A spontaneous order is inconceivable without personal freedom and, in particular, without freedom of choice. The socialist dream, on the other hand, depends for its realisation upon the limitation of the freedom of the individual, and the dilution of his sense of responsibility for his own acts.

We are always being told by the sociologist that it is impossible, even in theory, to separate the individual and society, and this is most certainly true when we are thinking in terms of human freedom. When people are persuaded to give up their freedom for the sake of the

43

community, or for some altruistic purpose like technological advance or economic growth, not only do they
lose their freedom: they are harming the cause, whatever it may be, that they are seeking to uphold.

3

It is sometimes said that the Conservative, who takes
pride above all in his practical approach to the problem
of man in society, is in fact as doctrinaire in his attitude
as the Socialist himself. Each, it can be argued, is at the
mercy of his own preconceptions; and the picture of a
society organised spontaneously by impersonal but on
the whole beneficent market forces, qualified by tradition and a sense of compassion, is neither more nor less
objective than the dream of a social system directed, in
the interests of the community, by an omniscient and
omnicompetent state.

In a narrow sense, no doubt, this kind of criticism can
be justified. The argument for a free against a planned
economy is concerned, certainly, with differences in economic theory. In any case, it is impossible altogether to
separate conviction from dogma. The important thing,
however, is not the form which a profession of faith
takes, but the foundation on which it rests. And the Conservative may reasonably claim that his own view of
society, and especially his view of human nature, is derived from experience, while that of the Socialist is based
on assumptions which may be true, indeed, but which
have never been put to the test or, when they have been,
have not survived it.

There are two assumptions, in particular, lying at the

44

core of progressive thought, which are altogether unsupported by experience, and which in themselves polarise the opposition of the socialist and the conservative outlook. They are, first, that man is a creature capable of unlimited improvement, moral as well as material, granted only that he has the right environment; and, secondly, that it is within the power of the state, as it is its duty, to create that environment.

This dangerous and demeaning delusion, that man can properly be regarded as raw material for the sociologist to mould as he thinks fit, has implications as absurd as they are terrifying. No one can say what will be the effect of the most carefully considered system of education upon a child. How, then, can it be possible to predict with any assurance at all the consequences of this kind of social engineering upon that infinitely more complex and baffling organism, human society?

But it is the sheer arrogance of the claim, not its inherent absurdity, which is alarming to the Conservative mind. Why, one asks, is it to be supposed that any group of people, no matter how intelligent or high-minded, is fitted to form the general character of a community of which it is so small a part? If it is given the power, what assurance is there that it will not abuse it? Above all, does not the appetite for power for these purposes indicate a view of humanity, and of the relationship between government and governed, which is utterly wrong? 'To manipulate men, to propel them towards goals which you—the social reformer—see, but they may not, is to deny their human essence, to treat them as objects without wills of their own, and therefore to degrade them.'*

* Isaiah Berlin, *Four Essays on Liberty,* Oxford University Press.

45

It is a marked characteristic of the Conservative that he does not, after all, believe that he is God, and for him, as for Burke, intellectual humility is the most prized quality in politics. As an essential precondition for the practice of his art, the statesman must realise that he is neither omniscient nor omnipotent; that he knows very little of the material that he has chosen to work in; and that he can ill judge in their totality the effect of his decisions upon it. It is this feeling for his own limitations, for his ignorance in the face of the mystery of life, his feeling, in short, for what Burke thought of as man's subordinate role in the long scheme of things, that chiefly distinguishes the Conservative.

Indeed, the intellectual position of the Conservative, when he surveys the vast immensity of the problems which face him, and the limited field of useful action which is open to him, is not unlike that of Mark Rutherford when he dreamed that he was preaching in St. Paul's: 'I pictured to myself the Cathedral full, and myself in the pulpit. I was excited when I imagined the opportunity offered me of delivering some message to the three or four thousand persons in such a building, but in a minute or two I discovered that my sermon would be very nearly as follows—"Dear friends, I know no more than you know; we had better go home".'*

This is not the kind of nightmare that is likely to disturb the slumbers of Mr. Harold Wilson or Mr. Richard Crossman, or of those who look to them for guidance. Nor is it the kind of thing that looks particularly well in an election manifesto. And yet it may be a more effective

* W. Hale White, *Mark Rutherford's Deliverance*.

launching pad for political action, by finite beings wrestling with problems of infinite complexity, than the intellectual Woomera from which the rockets of progressive thought are despatched into outer space.

CHAPTER III

BALDWINISM, BUTLERISM AND THE CONSENSUS

1

There is, then, an inevitable dichotomy between the progressive and the conservative view of life, between the humanist and the sceptic, between those who are conscious only of man's power and those who are aware, too, of his tragic and self-defeating weakness. And this confrontation expresses itself naturally in the parliamentary system. Indeed it is the essence of parliamentary government, and without the tension which it engenders Parliament itself declines, alike in its effectiveness and in the respect in which it is held.

In Britain, since 1939, there has grown up what has come to be called 'the consensus'. That is to say that instead of there being a clash between two parties with a different outlook and opposing philosophies, there is a field of agreement so wide that there is only a single approach to the major social and political problems of the day. Conservatives and Socialists alike have come to hold certain beliefs in common—for example that the raising of the material standard of life must be an absolute and overriding objective of government policy; and that if there is a surplus of spending power in the community, it should be exercised by the government on behalf of the citizen and not by the citizen for himself;

D

49

and that equality is an absolute good and class distinctions of any kind an absolute evil; and that the winning of a lottery is a piece of merited good fortune, but the enjoyment of investment income a kind of moral leprosy; and that institutions like parliamentary government, which have been developed over the centuries to meet one set of circumstances, and as the result of a particular political experience, can be transplanted among peoples whose circumstances and experience have been utterly different; and that there is no differentiation between cultures and civilisations, and that names are more important than the ideas they express. All of this has become common ground between the parties.

And all of these, and a dozen or two of similar propositions which are accepted without question by humane and responsible people, may be true. But they are not self-evident truths, and by persuading ourselves that they are we incur great risks. Not only may they be proved by experience to be ill-founded, or true only with such qualifications as to make them invalid for any practical purpose. The refusal to question them drains parliamentary debate, and political discussion generally, of all content. The party battle, a reality which sustains parliamentary government, becomes a sham fight which only weakens it. Party, the idea of men and women combining to advance principles and aspirations which they profess in common, is replaced by faction: the bond which unites party members is now no more than that which held together the Reds or the Greens in the circus at Constantinople. The choice is no longer between rival policies but only between two groups of men, or, increasingly, between two men. And as the idea of party is diluted, and the clash of party warfare becomes hollow and unreal, so Parliament itself falls in public esteem, and there is a growing cynicism about politicians and about the value of political discussion itself. The two-party system is replaced by a kind of one-party state.

The consensus, however, is no new thing in British politics. Its beginnings date back to the break-up of the Liberal party after the first world war and the emergence of the Labour party, dedicated to a revolutionary and extra-parliamentary creed, as the alternative government. The confusion so engendered had two consequences. First, the conflict between Liberal and Conservative, which had persisted since the days of the first Reform Bill, was brought to an abrupt end.

Of course the differences between the parties during the nineteenth century were not as clear cut as they seem to us today to have been. The picture we have of them is much influenced by the personal antagonism and mutual hatred of two parliamentarians of genius, Disraeli and Gladstone. It was a common criticism, made by Dickens among others, that the parliamentary battle was a sham battle. But the participants believed it to be a real one, and thought of themselves as fighting for causes in which they believed and which were real causes. With the break-up of the Liberal party in the first world war all this was changed. The party battle which had so furiously raged only a few years before was stilled. In its place there was an alliance between the more conservative elements in the Liberal party and the Conservative party itself. It had happened before, notably with the defection from Mr. Gladstone of a number of Liberals half a century earlier, on the Home Rule issue.

51

But this time the change was fundamental and it was irreversible. It was clear, from the moment, in December, 1916, when Asquith refused to serve under Lloyd George, that the Liberal party was finished as an effective parliamentary force and that it could never be renewed. The only thing in question now was the disposal of the assets.

This presented no problem for the Labour party, the natural heir of Liberal radicalism. But the Conservatives had to be up and doing to lay claim to their share of the estate, for they had no natural succession to it. Conservative policy must be slanted, therefore, towards those Liberal votes which might go one way or the other but of which a proportion could certainly be won over to the Conservative party by the appropriate appeal. This appeal was now no longer to tradition, or to anything which in the past had been thought of as specifically conservative. It was to anything and everything that might influence this unattached Liberal vote. It was no longer a matter of seeking to rally the country to a particular policy, but rather of finding a policy which would arouse the minimum of dissent. The character of party politics was being changed.

The emergence of the Labour party, itself the supplanter of the Liberals, blurred still further the edge of party controversy. While it was a condition of the effective working of Parliament that the clash between the parties should be a real one, reflecting genuine differences of principle, it was a condition also that the fight should not be à l'outrance. The game must be played according to the rules, and the two teams must play it on the same ground. In 1914, at the height of the Home

Rule controversy, these fundamental conditions seemed to be in doubt, even if it is not easy to apportion the blame, whether upon a Conservative opposition prepared to defy parliamentary convention to defend a minority, or upon a Liberal government ready to sacrifice that minority to fulfil a parliamentary bargain of which, to put the most charitable interpretation upon it, a subsidiary purpose was to maintain itself in office. Be that as it may, with the appearance, after the war of 1914, of the Labour party as the second party in the House of Commons, there was an entirely new situation. A parliamentary party of which the avowed aim was to do away with private property in all its forms, and which apparently owed its first allegiance to a foreign flag, was not covered by the rulebook. If the Labour party sincerely intended to carry out its declared policy, a Labour government with an overall parliamentary majority was a prospect too dangerous to be contemplated. And so it became the first aim of Conservative policy to prevent, or to stave off for as long as possible, so fearful a possibility. Beside this nothing else mattered.

Considerations of this kind, however, were entirely new to the idea of parliamentary government as it had been practised since the Reform Bill. Fifty or a hundred years ago the politician was as much interested in power as he is today, and as hungry for office. But generally speaking (and of course there were exceptions) it was office on his own terms that he was seeking, office on condition that he was empowered to give effect to the policies in which he believed—even if, like Salisbury, he did not believe in very much, or hope for very much. If this condition were not fulfilled, he was content to do without. It was not that he was a man of principle while his successors were without principle. He was playing the game according to the rules which he knew. When the Labour party appeared as the alternative government, the rules were changed.

2

The collapse of the Liberal party, then, and the emergence of Labour as the second party in the state, combined to produce what is sometimes known as Baldwinism. For it was Mr. Baldwin who, after a disastrous foray into the politics of principle with the general election of 1923 (an experience which he never forgot and which did much to shape his course during the years of power) substituted for a distinctive Conservative policy a policy deliberately designed to attract the widest possible measure of support from men of goodwill in all parties, in the Labour party as well as in the dying Liberal party. There is a very real difference between the two attitudes. It is no longer a matter of seeking to rally the country to a particular policy, conviction breeding conviction until at last one has brought a majority of one's fellow-subjects to one's side, but rather of propounding that policy which will provoke the least dissent.

This attitude of mind, if it was mistaken and led to disasters far greater than any that it averted, was not an unworthy one, and in two important respects Baldwin rendered his country a service which no other man, perhaps, could have done. His approach to social problems between the wars, and particularly during the 'twenties, and the educational process to which he submitted his

54

own party, meant that the social revolution which followed the second world war was accomplished without violence, and by general consent. And by putting off for so long the advent of a majority Labour government Baldwin gave time for a process of education, completed by the service of Labour ministers in the wartime coalition, which ensured that a Labour government, when it did come, was a responsible government even if it was not a conspicuously successful one.

It was in the field of foreign affairs, however, that the essential weakness of Baldwinism, and of what might be called the consensus approach to politics, was most evident. Baldwin was not attracted by foreign policy (or, indeed, by foreigners), and when at last in 1933 his interest was suddenly aroused, it was not because of what was happening abroad. It was because of what was happening at home—in the parliamentary constituency of East Fulham. And what was happening there interested him not for its effect on Europe, which was far more considerable than he ever knew, but for its effect upon the electoral prospects of the government of which he was the most powerful member. The wave of pacifism which swept over Britain at that time expressed itself suddenly and dramatically in the defeat of the Conservative candidate in what was thought to be an impregnable Conservative seat. Baldwin's reaction was less to educate a misguided public opinion than to demonstrate that his policy was attuned to it.

Baldwin was subsequently reported to have said that if he had told the people the truth about re-armament he would have lost the general election of 1935. He said no such thing. But he certainly played down re-armament,

55

and the dangers of the European situation, during the election. He feared, not without reason, that a Labour government if it had won the election would have jettisoned even the modest programme of re-armament which he was putting to the British people. He would have done better to speak plainly. It is possible that he would have been supported by the electorate; or that a Labour government, faced with the realities of the situation, would have reacted to them with vigour; or, if not, that it would have been replaced by another government with a clear mandate for re-armament. All this is speculation. What is certain is that the course which Baldwin adopted was the worst he could have chosen. It was trimmed and tailored to what people wanted to hear at a time when their whole future depended on their being told the truth. Baldwin was so obsessed by his search for the middle ground, for the consensus, that everything else, the safety of the country, the freedom of action of his successors, his own reputation, was sacrificed to it.

3

For Baldwin, however, there were mitigating circumstances which did not exist when the Conservative party was returned to power in 1951. By then the Liberal party was indisputably dead, and the Liberal vote, where it was not partially neutralised by the intervention of a Liberal candidate, was gathered into the barn, on one side or the other. The prospect of a majority Labour government was not an ominous threat on the horizon. The threat had already materialised, and to stave it off was no longer the first consideration. The gaining of power as an end in itself could be subordinated, once more, to the uses to which power, once gained, was to be put. Once more it was possible for the Conservative party to base policy upon conviction. But the opportunity was allowed to pass.

After their victory in 1964 Socialists delighted to speak of 'the thirteen wasted years' of Conservative government. There was more in the jibe than those at whom it was directed were prepared to admit. Instead of consolidating the social advances which had been achieved by the post-war Labour government, or modifying them when modification was clearly necessary, its successors only extended them. Instead of reforming a system of public expenditure and taxation demoralising to the citizen and burdensome to industry and enterprise, Conservative governments were content to continue the levelling tendencies of their predecessors, and successive chancellors of the exchequer seemed more concerned to check tax-avoidance than to ease the burden of taxation. And looking out on a world in which British power had faded and shrunk, a Conservative government made no effort to restore it. It could do no more than bend suppliant before the wind of change, which it had done so much itself to conjure up, repeating the facile shibboleths of progressive thought, and adding its own authority to the pretence that words are more important than facts; that Commonwealth is more respected than Empire; and that something called moral influence is an effective substitute for power. By the time another Labour government was called to office, half of its programme had been realised, and most of its claims endorsed, by its predecessor.

57

That things turned out like this was due in the main to two factors—the effect upon the Conservative party of the wartime coalition, and the character of the party leadership after the war.

That England has no love for coalitions is a truism that by now hardly bears repeating. There are solid grounds, nevertheless, for her mistrust. Coalition, from its very nature, means that honest differences of opinion are suppressed. The emergency which creates it ensures, while the coalition lasts, that its maintenance is an overriding objective of policy. These considerations applied to what Sir Winston Churchill, with justifiable pride, called the Great Coalition. Without it, victory would not have been achieved; but it could not have survived without some sacrifice of principle. And for a number of reasons—that Conservatism is less dogmatic and more flexible than Socialism; that the Conservative gives a higher priority to considerations of national defence; and that the Conservative is less concerned with the future and more with the imperatives of the present—it was the principles of the Conservatives, not those of the Labour party, that went to the wall. Thus the Conservative party emerged from the Coalition, not only without any distinctive policy (apart from the claim to superior leadership in the person of Churchill) but without any distinctive convictions.

When the Conservative party went into opposition in 1945, and even when it returned to office after six years in the wilderness, there was a sense in which it could be said that the leadership was in commission. Of course Churchill towered over his colleagues, who were scarcely visible in his mighty shadow. No leader since the youn-

ger Pitt—not Disraeli, not Gladstone, not Lloyd George
—had ever commanded such authority. But he did not
always choose, nor was he always able, to exercise it. He
was by now an old man, and his genius, only fitful now,
was absorbed by the tremendous and novel tendencies
which were beginning to disclose themselves in history.
It was with reluctance that he brought himself to face
what were, for him, the minutiae of economic and social
policy, and when he did so his touch was uncertain and it
almost seemed that he, too, was obsessed with his 'image'
(as though that were necessary) and with the need to
show that he was not the Churchill of Sydney Street or
Tonypandy or the *British Gazette*.

At this point in his career Churchill was like an in-
verted Baldwin, bringing to international affairs all the
resolution with which Baldwin turned his back on them.
And if he was obliged to give a decision on some domestic issue, the standards to which he referred were not
those of a Conservative. In spite of his great sense of
history, and the fact that he had opened his political
career as a Conservative member of Parliament, Churchill was not and had never been a Conservative. In his
dealings with the Conservative party, even after he became its leader—especially after he became its leader—
he was never completely at ease. He was inclined, where
his own interest and sympathies were not engaged, to
defer to those who might be supposed to have deeper
sympathy with party feeling. There was a wide range of
subjects, immensely important in themselves but not so
regarded by Churchill, on which he was prepared to take
advice. And this advice was not always well-founded.

4

There was thus a gap in the structure of the Conservative party. It was filled by Mr. R. A. Butler. When the party went into opposition after the war Mr. Butler was given control of that part of the organisation which concerned itself with the development of policy. It was a task for which, in all respects save one, he was eminently fitted; it was a task, too, to which none of the first rank of the party felt an especial call. And when, on the formation of Churchill's 1951 government, Mr. Butler became Chancellor of the Exchequer, his influence on domestic policy was second only to that of the Prime Minister himself. In some respects, indeed, his influence was decisive. And certainly it was his image, rather than Churchill's, which stamped itself on the post-war Conservative party.

This was not wholly fortunate. Mr. Butler, unlike Churchill, was a Conservative; but his was a special brand of Conservatism, equivocal, a little ambiguous, calculated less to attract support than to avoid offence. Mr. Butler, who as a young man had held junior but still responsible office under Baldwin, was in a special sense heir to the Baldwin tradition. More than any of his contemporaries, all of whom had come under the magician's influence—and only those who were exposed to it can have any idea of its magic—he was an exponent of Baldwinism, seeing at all times the middle of the road, seeking at all times for the widest measure of agreement, searching always for the one sinner that repenteth and always forgetting the ninety and nine who have no need of repentance but who manage somehow to keep the wheels turning.

But to the old tradition Mr. Butler added an especial gloss of his own. Where Baldwin used a wide brush on a broad canvas, with sweeping strokes that went straight from the eye to the heart, Mr. Butler favoured the tools of the engraver. Calculation and subtlety were substituted for warmth and sympathy. Whatever his audience, Baldwin's appeal was still to tradition, to patriotism, to the essential Englishry at the core of the Englishman's heart. Mr. Butler's was rather to his brain, an organ which, with the Englishman, has never been decisive for action. One could not imagine Mr. Baldwin telling one of his St. George's Day audiences that, by taking thought, they could double their standard of living within twenty-five years.

And there was another marked difference between the two men. Mr. Baldwin, with his naturally cultivated mind, saturated in English history and the English tongue, was essentially unintellectual—or perhaps anti-intellectual would better fit his attitude of mind, for his contempt for what he called the intelligentzia was without bounds. But one of Mr. Butler's most marked characteristics (and one that influenced greatly his political attitudes) was his desire to stand well with that part of the intellectual establishment which tends to be 'progressive', forward-looking and anti-conservative.

Thus it was that the Conservative party which emerged after the defeat of 1945 was shaped to carry on a tradition already outdated and discredited.

It has often been said that without the process of education which Mr. Butler imposed on the Conserva-

tive party, and without the blood transfusion to which
he submitted it, the party could never have won the
general election of 1951. But the election was not won by
the Conservative party. It was lost by the Labour party,
rejected by an electorate wearied and exasperated by the
continuation, through five years of peace, of the restric-
tions of wartime. In so far as the public responded to the
Conservative appeal (as distinct from reacting against
the Socialist government), it was not to Mr. Butler and
his Industrial Charter but to Mr. Churchill's clear call:
'Set the people free!'

It is equally a mistake to suppose that Mr. Butler, re-
deeming the party from the errors of reaction and
obscurantism, brought it out of the shadows of the past, a
modern party acceptable to a modern electorate. Even
by the end of the war the character of the Conservative
party had changed. The men who were in control during
the twenty years between the wars, and whose political
outlook had been formed in the very different world of
Victorian or Edwardian England, had left the stage. For
the first time those who had taken part in the first world
war, or who had grown to manhood after it, were, subject only to Churchill's dominating influence, at the very
centre of power.

But the war had brought about other changes. These
were a new spirit abroad, and a determination that the
experiences of the war, and the spirit which it had
evoked, should not be wasted. There was a sense of
obligation that a new society should be created, free of
the blemishes which had disfigured the England of the
'thirties. From these feelings Conservatives were not ex-
empted, for they too were human. The danger was not

62

that the Conservative party would prove too reactionary, but that it would be carried so far along the road of change as to lose the characteristics which would enable it, in due course, to make its distinctive contribution to the creation of the new society. And this is what happened. All that the party had to offer, in the wasted years, was a reformulation of the fashions of the day.

CHAPTER IV

THE MYTH OF THE MIDDLE GROUND

I

The tendency of the modern Conservative party to reflect passing fashion rather than any coherent principle
of government—a consequence of the confusion into
which the party system was thrown after the first world
war—was disastrously reinforced, after the second, by
the development of psephology. This new science (or
mystery, for there is not much that is scientific about it)
is concerned with analysis of election results, from which
it purports to deduce conclusions about the behaviour of
the electorate in general. These claims, however, are
pitched too high. Like the Home Office pathologist con-
ducting a post-mortem, the psephologist can tell us what
has happened. With sampling techniques and the help
of a computer, he can even anticipate, by some hours,
voting trends before they are clearly established. But
that is the limit of his power over the future. He can no
more say what causes the voter to react in one way rather
than another to a political stimulus, than the pathologist, is able, by an examination of the organs of a corpse,
to pronounce on the state of mind of the poisoner.

There has grown up around the statistical analysis of
election results, nevertheless, a whole system of general-
isations which, rightly interpreted, is supposed to give
infallible guidance to the politician in his bid for elec-

E   65

toral support. It amounts to no more than this: there is a number of voters who can be relied upon to support one of two parties, and a number, more or less equal, which will support the other, while a third group, less numerous than either, tips the balance and decides the issue. This is the army of the uncommitted, the 'don't knows' who, between elections, figure somewhat ignominiously at the bottom of the opinion polls. That party, then, which is able to carry this middle ground, to attract this floating vote, will win the day.

This is a plausible and in some ways an attractive theory, for it greatly simplifies the politician's task. It is only necessary to decide what the uncommitted voter wants, and to give it to him. There is no need to consider the tastes or the predilections of the party stalwart for he, poor soul, has nowhere else to go. This central redoubt, the stronghold of uncommitted opinion, can be captured by direct assault, provided only that the attacking troops are so disguised as to be indistinguishable from the defenders. This, no doubt, is what people have in mind when they say that 'politics is about the centre', an aphorism which has greatly influenced the Conservative party in recent years, and which conceals a number of assumptions of doubtful validity, some of them quite amoral and some only absurd. It assumes that decisions are normally taken, in a democratic society, by a minority, and a small minority, of those concerned; or, alternatively, that this minority somehow reflects the real wishes of the majority as the majority itself cannot reflect them; or, again, that it is in some sense the repository of the judgement and experience of the whole electorate as the electorate itself is not.

But there is another assumption, equally curious and no more easily justified: that this uncommitted élite, at once all powerful and all wise, and without party allegiance of any kind, is definitely progressive and anti-conservative in its outlook. In fact it is committed after all. And so the floating voter, not quite so buoyant as he was at first thought to be, must be shielded, at almost any cost in terms of convictions sacrificed and freedom of action compromised, from anything that might give offence to him. The implication is clear. Policies which in themselves command wide backing, or which, at the least, ought to be the subject of public debate, have to be suppressed for fear of repelling a minority on whose support office is thought to depend. It is certainly a very curious interpretation of democracy.

But there is another consideration which is relevant. Why don't the 'Don't Knows' know? A proportion of them, perhaps the greater proportion, don't know because they don't care: they go to make up that percentage which, even at the most hotly contested election, does not bother to vote. Of the rest, are we really justified in assuming that they are a body of disinterested and public-spirited citizens, carefully balancing argument with argument and advantage with disadvantage, until finally, and out of an unusual concern for the public good, they come down on one side or the other? And even if this assumption is justified, why do we suppose that they are all influenced by the same considerations, that they will all be attracted, or offended, by the same policies?

There is another and equally plausible hypothesis. It is that the 'uncommitted voter' is nothing more than the

party voter who, disenchanted with his own, has no inclination to support the opposite party. Commenting on
the general election of 1955, the compiler of the *Annual
Register* for that year concludes that the uncommitted
voter is sufficiently rare to be unimportant, and that that
party wins which brings its own supporters to the polls.*
If this is so, the whole elaborate system of political
strategy which is based upon the need to win over the
uncommitted voter is not only unnecessary: it is self-
defeating, too.

2

Leaving aside, for the time being, the question of
whether the uncommitted vote is as important as it is
thought to be or whether it is necessary to submit to its
pressures, it is worth considering some of the consequences of such a surrender. The deference which is
customarily shown by the Conservative leadership to the
uncommitted vote, that central redoubt which is
thought to be the ultimate repository of political power,
has resulted in a form of censorship which is none the
less real, and no less damaging, because no one recognises it for what it is.

The subject of race relations is a case in point. The
Labour Government of 1945 introduced, as some sort of
compensation for the loss of the British Empire, legislation of which the effect was to give citizenship of the
United Kingdom to all the erstwhile subjects of that
empire. The privileges which were thus extended were
not reciprocated, and the British Nationality Act

* *Annual Register*, 1955. p. 31.

68

reflected no kind of reality: it was as though the principle 'Civis Romanus Sum' had been enunciated for the
first time after the sack of Rome by Alaric. But it was by
no means an empty gesture, for it opened the way for
unlimited immigration into Great Britain from the
coloured Commonwealth.

The consequences of this ill-considered piece of legislation did not, however, make themselves immediately
apparent, and it was only later, with a Conservative
government in office, that the nature, and the magnitude, of the problem became evident. With a com-
placency which seems scarcely intelligible today, that
government watched a trickle become a flood, without
seeming to understand that it was deliberately, as a
matter of policy, importing into this country a problem
which, for the second time in a hundred years, was
tearing the United States apart, and from which, until
now, we ourselves had been free.

It is not easy today to see into the minds of the leaders
of the Conservative party ten and fifteen years ago. They
supposed, no doubt, that they were giving some sort of
reality to the illusion that the new 'Commonwealth' was
an effective substitute for the old Empire. They argued
that they were relieving a labour shortage in this country, particularly in the National Health Service, but they
scarcely seemed to realise that in doing so they were rob-
bing the new Commonwealth countries of the few doctors and technicians they possessed. Above all, perhaps,
they thought of themselves as displaying a degree of
enlightenment and proper feeling of which the old-
fashioned Conservative would have been incapable.

And as the difficulties created by the flood of new

immigrants began to disclose themselves in the succeeding decade, there was a general and probably inevitable
tendency in political circles to pretend that they did not
exist. On the one side, the Labour party considered itself
to be in an especial sense the champion and defender of
the under-privileged (for as such the new immigrants
were immediately classified). On the other, the Conservative leadership, reluctant to draw attention to the consequences of its own lack of foresight, was unwilling to
incur the further odium of an attitude which might be
criticised as being 'illiberal' by central and uncommitted
opinion. With both sides agreed, although for very
different reasons, that silence was golden, it was natural
that criticism should be muted, and public discussion of
a serious social problem, of concern to every citizen, be
looked upon as a kind of indecency. But although it was
natural it was unhealthy, and it was politically very
dangerous. For as the normal safety valves of discussion
and debate were closed, so the tensions created by the
large-scale immigration of coloured people of an alien
culture began to increase.

This was the situation to which Mr. Enoch Powell,
whose constituency of East Wolverhampton was one of
the foci of the problem, and who had, on that account,
an especial knowledge of its impact, had been drawing
attention long before the speech at Birmingham which
created what came to be known as 'Powellism'. But what
makes Powellism a disturbing phenomenon in English
public life is not its effect upon coloured immigration.
That, on balance, has been salutary, because it has compelled politicians of both parties to admit the reality of a
problem which they had found it much more comfort-

able to ignore. Of this the extent to which the attitude of Conservatives and Socialists alike has been modified or made explicit since Mr. Powell made his speech is clear enough proof. What is disturbing is the light which it throws upon the attitudes, essentially illiberal, of those who regard themselves, and were once regarded, as being especially the guardians of the liberal tradition.

It cannot be said that Mr. Enoch Powell is the first politician, expressing unpopular views, who has been shouted down. What is certain is that no politician of Mr. Powell's intellectual distinction and integrity has ever before been consistently howled down in centres of learning. And in some cases this behaviour, which runs counter to everything for which a university is supposed to stand, has been supported and encouraged by the university authorities themselves. If parliamentary government is under threat it is not difficult to see from where the threat comes.*

It is indeed curious that at a time when any kind of moral censorship is thought to be eccentric almost to the point of indecency, and when the most intimate of human relationships are regarded as fit subjects for pub-

---

* The Principal and Vice-Chancellor of the University of Dundee is reported in the press (*Daily Telegraph*, 18 October 1969) as having decided to 'support counter tactics' to prevent Mr. Enoch Powell from addressing a meeting of the University Conservative Association. And some little time ago a leading television personality, speaking from the pulpit of St. Paul's Cathedral, delivered himself of the aphorism: 'All Powellism corrupts, but absolute Powellism corrupts absolutely.' The speaker must have heard of Lord Acton although he can scarcely have read him. Neither the Church nor the Faith of which it is the custodian, will ever regain its influence by encouraging this kind of exhibitionism.

lic examination, the discussion of political questions should be subjected to a rigorous censorship, and this in a country which has always prided itself on its political sophistication. It seems as though human nature has a positive need for taboos, and that when they are extirpated from the soil in which they naturally grow, they take root again where they do far more harm.

3

But the search for the middle ground in politics is questionable not only because it leads to an unacknowledged censorship. It has other implications which are equally undesirable. As the Conservatives found after the election of 1935, it can be more than embarrassing, it can be highly dangerous when a government finds its freedom of action limited by undertakings given in order to obtain the power to act. And there is the further implication, no more admirable, that the only function of a political party is to govern, and its only duty to gain power irrespective of the uses to which power is to be put. Opposition is regarded as no more than an interlude, a springboard from which to leap into office once again.

But this is not so. A parliamentary party has another duty, a continuing one and in the long run, perhaps, a more important one. It is, alike in office and in opposition, to influence the social climate in general by expressing its own philosophy in a coherent and consistent form. When the party veers and wavers, not in response to public opinion but only in order to create an 'image' calculated to impress favourably a progressive and sup-

72

posedly influential élite, it is abrogating this most important function and, in the belief that it is raising it, is lowering the general level of public life.

The imposition of a capital gains tax by a Conservative Chancellor of the Exchequer, for example, not in substitution for existing imposts but as an addition to them, might be thought unbecoming in a party which professes its faith in the efficacy of the profit motive as an economic and social stimulus. There were other and more useful things to be done—a reform of the taxation system, a scrutiny of public expenditure or an examination of the social and even the moral implications of the welfare state in an affluent society. While the new tax was designed to appeal to the voter in the middle of the road who is supposed, *ex hypothesi*, to be suspicious of profits, there is no evidence whatever to suggest that it influenced him to support the Conservative party. Its only effect was to intensify the egalitarian atmosphere which it is the purpose of Socialism to create, and to facilitate the next step towards a restrictive and repressive equality.

Again, a reforming Home Secretary in a Conservative government can do nothing which a progressive cannot do better, but by doing it he weakens the fabric of conviction which is the ultimate justification of party government. The reform of the Gaming Acts may or may not have been desirable, but a Conservative Home Secretary would have been wiser to strengthen the structure of law and order than to impose greater strain upon it.

In the same way, the uncommitted and non-commital attitude, in opposition, of the Conservative leadership towards the social reforms of the nineteen-sixties—the abolition of the death penalty, the abolition of censorship in the theatre, the relaxation of the law on obscenity, the reform of the laws relating to sexual offences and abortion—reflected a deference to minority opinion, and a fear of offending it, which it is difficult to justify on democratic or any other grounds.

The Member of Parliament, part welfare officer and part censor not so much of morals as of opinion, but no longer a representative of the commons of England, does not hesitate, on those questions which he thinks ought, as the saying goes, to be 'taken out of politics', to oppose himself to the known wishes of his constituents. It is a curious constitutional theory that an electorate, supposedly capable of forming a judgement on the most abstruse of economic and political problems, should be thought unfitted to pronounce on matters where the ordinary experience of human life weighs as much as any expert opinion. It is likely, indeed, that a Member of Parliament in the days of a restricted franchise represented more truly the views of ordinary men and women than he does today, perhaps because he understood better his fellow-countrymen.

There is little doubt that majority opinion in the country was opposed to the social reforms of the 'sixties, and conservative opinion overwhelmingly so. The minority, perhaps, was more enlightened, but it was still a minority. And it carried the day not because it was enlightened but because it was thought to represent that influential central opinion which decides elections.

As with any sweeping changes, these reforms, in their totality, had consequences which most certainly were not

74

intended by those Conservatives, at any rate, who voted for them. In fact there could be no better example of the danger, so clearly seen by Burke, of meddling light-heartedly with the delicate, mysterious and imperfectly understood structure of society.

4

The Labour party has never let itself be gulled into the belief that it is possible to convert the unconverted simply by agreeing with him. On the contrary. At the 1960 conference of the Labour party, Mr. Gaitskell endeavoured to delete from the party constitution the famous Clause 4, which ties the Labour party to the principle of 'the nationalisation of the means of production, distribution and exchange'. This seemed to him to be no longer relevant. Here his judgement was certainly sound. He thought, too, that it had the effect of scaring away the uncommitted voter on whom the party must depend if it were ever again to form a government. But here he was wrong. The conference would have none of this Butskellism.* It rejected Mr. Gaitskell's proposal. The uncommitted voter was not frightened off, and the Labour party won the next general election. The rank and file of the party, who had to carry the battle to the street corners and the terraces, understood what their leader lacked the experience to know—that you do not disarm your enemy by pretending to agree with him: you only dishearten and demoralise your own side.

* The term which was applied to the apparent agreement on most issues between Mr. Butler, the leader of the House of Commons, and Mr. Gaitskell, the leader of the opposition.

In the final analysis it is the zeal of the army, its faith in itself and its commander, that wins over the deserters and the waverers. Conviction, not the desire to please, creates support.

In sober truth, the middle ground in politics, the Eldorado of the psephologist and those who pin their faith to him, lacks all reality. Like a mirage, it vanishes as you approach it. There is many a disillusioned candidate who has come to understand, as he watches the votes being counted, that his anxiety to gain the respect of his opponents has gained him nothing else, and has only lost him the support of his friends. This was something that the old Lord Salisbury knew well.

'His correspondence during this period (1891–92) included, naturally, many suggestions from different quarters for "popular" items to be added to the party's programme. They were replied to in diverse ways but he constantly recurred to his old contention that "as a question of electoral arithmetic", as he put it, the party would lose more by alarming its normal supporters than it would ever gain by bidding for the gratitude of those who were not. . . . "You may say that they cannot vote against you, but they won't trouble to vote for you and they won't work for you, and you'll find it out at the polls." He attributed the loss of this election (1892) as a whole largely to that cause.'*

It is not easy for those Conservatives who have never contested parliamentary elections, or who have never

* Lady Gwendolen Cecil: *Life of Robert, Marquis of Salisbury*, Vol. IV, pp. 401–2.

fought in difficult working class constituencies, to grasp the truth that electioneering is at least as much a moral as it is a political exercise, and that success depends more on the power of leadership to inspire the party worker so that he, in his turn, convinces the waverer, than on its capacity to persuade the waverer by argument. When all is said, the floating vote lives up to its name. It floats with the tide; and whoever would influence it must first influence the tide.

CHAPTER V

THE CONSERVATIVE ABROAD

1

The weakness in the Conservative leadership, which expressed itself in the urge at all costs to follow political fashion rather than to influence it, covered the whole field of politics. It was more understandable, however, in relation to foreign affairs, where there has been an upheaval so violent that there was an absolute lack of guide lines to which to refer or of experience on which to draw, than at home.

Changes in the balance of power, military and economic, consequent upon two world wars; the sudden and unforeseen confrontation of the United States and the Soviet Union at a level of power which no other nation on earth could challenge; and the re-appearance of China upon the world scene after centuries of eclipse, brought down the curtain, overnight as it were, upon Britain's long-sustained role as a world power. And it was not only Britain that was affected. Europe, the cradle of western civilisation, was no longer the centre of the world. As Henry the Navigator, watching from his tower at Sagres and turning his back upon the Mediterranean Sea, saw a new world at the end of the Atlantic trade routes, so, four hundred years later, men began to look towards the Pacific on whose shores something new again was beginning to stir.

But that was not all. There was a new element in the problem which, especially for Britain, increased immeasurably its complexity. This was the development of the nuclear bomb. It was not only that Britain, like the rest of the world, stood at risk of annihilation. She found herself impaled on the horns of a cruel dilemma. If she did not possess her own nuclear deterrent, an independent policy was impossible for her. If she did possess it, the strain on her economy and her technical resources would one day become insupportable.

Britain, moreover, could have her own deterrent, and the capacity to deliver it, only by grace of the United States, and although this was conceded, it was conceded unwillingly, as one yields to the importunity of an old friend. For it was one of Washington's cardinal purposes—as real, and more realistic than its preoccupation with colonialism—to prevent the proliferation of nuclear weapons; and British insistence upon an independent deterrent, her demand for 'a seat at the top table', ran directly counter to American policy, as it was probably against Britain's own interests. In truth there was no real option for Britain. As nuclear weapons and delivery systems became more sophisticated, so the cost escalated; and it was completely unrealistic to suppose that the United States government would indefinitely support a policy which it thought to be positively dangerous. For Britain the nuclear road could only be, in the end, a blind alley.

None of this was the fault of the Conservative party. It

arose out of the facts. And if the party mistook their implications, it was not alone in this. The Labour party,
too, misread the portents. Relying upon a theory of internationalism insufficiently substantial to prevail
against the supposed interests of the trades unions, and
at the same time following the will o' the wisp of nuclear
independence, it turned its back upon Europe at the
very moment when the leadership of a United Europe
might have been had for the asking, and a Treaty of
London have taken the place of the Treaty of Rome. But
Britain's changed position in a changed world affected
especially the Conservative party which had been bred
to the idea of Empire, and for which independence, not
internationalism, was in the nature of a political, indeed
a moral, imperative.

It was not surprising that the party leaders, seeking for
some path through the wilderness of the post-war world,
wavered between a United Europe of which this country
might be the cornerstone, a Commonwealth which could
both support and influence the United Nations, and a
'special relationship' with the United States.

Nothing expresses more clearly the innate contradic-
tions in Conservative policy than the varying attitudes of
the party leaders towards Europe and the European
Community. In the years of opposition between 1945
and 1951, Churchill urged Franco-German reconciliation as a step towards 'a kind of United States of Europe'
and proposed the 'immediate creation of a European
Army under a unified command in which we should all
bear a working and an honourable part'. I can remember listening to him in the House of Commons, in the
spring of 1950, when he urged that Frenchmen, English-

F   81

men and Germans should 'make the core of a nucleus upon which all the other civilised democracies of Europe . . . can rally and combine', so that in the mid-twentieth century 'the grand design of Charlemagne' could be re-adapted to modern conditions.

I heard nearly every speech that Churchill made in Parliament from 193▶ onwards, and I can think of none more profoundly moving, not even the war speeches, than this one. It moved me because this old man, behind him a lifetime of action and adventure, of failure and defeat, of success and victory, of despair and triumph, turned his back on it all to look forward with the eyes of a boy, at the beginning of life, to a future that he would never see. 'Your old men shall dream dreams, and your young men shall see visions.' It was this inversion of Joel's prophecy that was so remarkable and so touching. And yet it was only rhetoric after all. For Churchill, too, was a split personality, torn between Europe and the Atlantic, and in some way confused by his conception of the three interlocking circles, of Europe, Empire and North America.*

At Columbia University in January, 1952, Anthony Eden, Foreign Secretary in Churchill's Ministry, spoke as follows:

'Britain's story and her interests lie far beyond the Continent of Europe. Our thoughts move across the seas to the many countries in which our people play their part, in every corner of the world. These are our family ties. That is our life: without it we should be no more than some millions of people living on an

* House of Commons, March, 1950.

island off the coasts of Europe, in which nobody wants to take any particular interest.'

Où sont les neiges d'antan? Where now are these many communities in every part of the world in which our people play their part?

'We will allow no supranational authority to put large masses of our people out of work in Durham, in the Midlands, in South Wales or in Scotland.'*

It is Harold Macmillan who speaks, the same Macmillan who, not so long after, led the first unsuccessful attempt to take Britain into Europe. And on the other side, the Labour government declared that 'a political federation, limited to Western Europe, is not compatible either with our Commonwealth ties, our obligations as a member of the wider Atlantic community, or as a world power'.* Again, it was not long before another Labour government was hammering vainly at the doors of the Common Market.

To listen today to these echoes from the past is less to wonder at the lack of foresight of our leaders (for which of us saw things any more clearly?) than to understand the suddenness as well as the magnitude of the changes which had overtaken Britain's position in the world. And when, a little later, Mr. Dean Acheson said of us that we had lost an empire without finding a role, he was not so much expressing a criticism as explaining the atmosphere of confusion, uncertainty and self-doubt into which the swift current of events had carried us. We

* Quoted by George W. Ball, *The Discipline of Power*, pp. 75–6.

were torn by conflicting aims—the leadership of a new Europe, the leadership of a Commonwealth from which the virtue had departed, and the continuing hope of a special relationship with the United States.

But the 'special relationship', to the extent that it was still a reality, was a relationship not a policy, not even a basis for a policy. During the second war the exigencies of the situation led to a partnership between the governments of the United States and the United Kingdom, not only in military matters; it was even more real, perhaps, in the field of supply and in the general economic conduct of the war. Over a wide area it could almost be said that there were not two governments but one, and there came to be established, especially at the official level, a degree of confidence and trust which was unique; and this has persisted, in greater or less degree, ever since.*

But with the end of the war two things happened. It was impossible, and probably undesirable, for the partnership to remain exclusive, even if there was a tendency on the British side to try to keep it so. And it became evident as events unfolded that this unique relationship was essentially personal rather than political. It depended very largely upon the degree of confidence which existed between individual members of the two governments. The 'special relationship' was not a firm

* I was fortunate enough to have some experience of this myself when I made frequent visits to Washington as a member of Churchill's government. The distinction between officials and politicians is always somewhat blurred in Washington, and it was exhilarating to discuss current problems with members of the Administration as freely as one would with one's colleagues or advisers at home.

political alliance based on a common and world-wide view of events; indeed it concealed deep divisions of policy and intention. But the belief that things were otherwise, and that there was a common purpose under-lying the relationship between the two countries, while it did not affect the picture that Britain presented to the world, distorted the image that she saw in the mirror, thus making it harder for her to reach an accommodation with reality. The shock was all the greater, there-fore, when the limitations of the special relationship be-came apparent with the Suez crisis in 1956.

2

This is not the place to attempt an analysis of what has come to be known, in the cant of the day, as 'the Suez adventure', or to apportion responsibility between a President without political experience and ignorant of history; a Secretary of State at Washington lacking in candour and directness; and a Prime Minister watching from London the foundations of what he thought to be a common policy being sapped, day after day and week after week, by the deviousness of an ally. But this much can be said: the failure to organise any international action to reverse a unilateral act of depredation, and the constitutional and ingrained inability of the United Nations to reach an objective appraisal of the situation, led directly to the condition of continuing anarchy which has persisted in the Middle East ever since.*

* It might be salutary, nevertheless, if those who so freely criticise Sir Anthony Eden were to read again the speech in which the leader of the opposition denounced in the House of Commons not the British but the Egyptian adventurer: 'The French Prime

For Britain it had another consequence. It made it the more imperative—or so it seemed—that she should have her own deterrent. It was not a question now of 'a seat at the top table', a matter of prestige or influence. If it had not been clear before, it was clear after Suez that the United States would not be prepared to see New York, Chicago or Los Angeles wiped off the map in order to protect London. If an independent deterrent had been desirable before as an instrument of policy, it seemed now to be the condition of survival.

It would have been impossible, amid the secular changes occurring in the world and with the agonising nature of the choices which were open to him, for any British statesman to follow a coherent and consistent policy. But one of the consequences of Suez was that the British people had a shock, traumatic in its effect, from which they have not yet fully recovered. It was not only that they suffered a total defeat and that the narrowness of the limits which had now been set to British power was brought home to them as never before, but also the

---

Minister, M. Mollet, the other day quoted a speech of Colonel Nasser's and rightly said that it could remind us only of one thing—of the speeches of Hitler before the war.... It is exactly the same that we encountered from Mussolini and Hitler in those years before the war.' Hugh Gaitskell, *Hansard*, 1956, Vol. 557, columns 1612/1613.

At that point, at any rate, it is clear that in the eyes of the leader of the Labour party, Colonel Nasser was the aggressor. In fairness to Mr. Gaitskell it must be added that he made it clear in the same speech that any action against Colonel Nasser must be through the United Nations. As the United Nations could not or would not take action, the policy of the Labour party was to say the least of it sterile: the party was back among the illusions of the 'thirties when, with equal fervour, it attacked the government of the day for not 'standing up to the dictators' while it refused it the arms which would have made defiance possible.

fact that they found themselves the target of a world-wide campaign of obloquy against which scarcely a voice was raised in protest, created feelings of guilt, almost obsessional in their intensity, which shattered their self-confidence and distorted their view of the world about them and their place in it.

The differences between the British and American governments at the time of Suez were political and practical and not, as they are usually represented to have been, differences in moral attitudes. And this is true despite the Israeli invasion of Egypt. The collusive concealment which preceded the invasion was perhaps immoral. Perhaps it was ill-judged. Perhaps, and this is most likely, it was inevitable, given the characters of the protagonists, and the situation in which they were bound to each other. The crisis developed with that kind of tragic necessity which haunts the doom-laden ruins of Agamemnon's palace at Mycenae. What is known as the Suez adventure ought more properly to be thought of as the Suez tragedy.*

But for Sir Anthony Eden and Mr. Selwyn Lloyd, at any rate, the Suez crisis was essentially a question of how to reverse an act of naked aggression which, unchecked, would lead to further aggression. The case is best put, perhaps, by an American writing five years afterwards: 'The British, despoiled in Egypt, as we have been in Cuba, were pilloried for defending their rights under international law. . . . No wonder that this doctrine has led to the general breakdown of whatever respect for law survived the nineteenth century.'† For Mr. Secretary

*See Herman Finer, *Dulles Over Suez*, especially pp. 324–410.
† Dean Acheson, op. cit.

Dulles the problem was more complex. In part because of his ambivalent attitude, half bluster and half fear, towards the Soviet Union; partly to safeguard the position of the United States in relation to the Panama Canal; and partly to underline a permanent principle in American policy, Mr. Dulles had to demonstrate that the United States, in spite of being Britain's ally for other purposes and in other regions, dissociated itself entirely from British 'colonialism' for this particular purpose and in this particular region. But because so many people told them so, the British began to think of themselves as the basest of criminals, and of the United Nations as a judgement seat, manned and staffed by celestial beings, free of all earthly passions, dispensing to all who sought it an impartial and even-handed justice. They did not see it for what it was, a political arena where the communist countries sided with the 'emergent' to undermine or pillage the western world—and where, on this occasion, it was the United States that led the pack.*

Looking back, it is certainly one of the most astonishing features of the Suez crisis that when it was over no voice was raised in defence of British policy, even by those who shared the responsibility for it. The new Prime Minister, himself a protagonist in the tragedy, was intent upon sweeping the whole affair under the carpet, and for this there was more than one reason. Most com-

* The effects of Suez were not confined to the Middle East and Africa. The long and tortuous process by which Mr. Dulles managed to free himself from any commitment to his allies, and the President's utter lack of comprehension of what was happening, were a serious blow to the integrity of the North Atlantic Treaty Organisation itself. It suggested to others besides General de Gaulle, watching from the wings, that in the last resort American policy was unpredictable and not to be relied upon.

88

pelling was the need to undo, as far as it was possible to undo it, the harm that had been done to Anglo-American relations, and this not in the interests of the two countries alone but for the good of the North Atlantic alliance in general. But there was another reason, perhaps less creditable and certainly less soundly based. Although the Suez operation commanded general public support, and although the enforced evacuation, and the circumstances attending it, aroused much resentment, that supposedly influential élite which occupies the central ground and which is thought, however mistakenly, to hold the key to electoral success, was opposed to it. At all costs this body of opinion must be placated and appeased.

And because there has never been any public debate on the real issues raised by Suez, the wrong conclusions were drawn from the crisis. It was thought that because Britain had not the power to impose her will upon the United States, she could have no will of her own anywhere. It was thought, because the United Nations had delivered judgement against Britain, that the United Nations possessed an unassailable moral authority. It was thought that if former colonial territories gained their 'independence' they acquired with it all the attributes of a modern nation state, and that their voices would be as authoritative, and in a moral sense more compelling than those of societies which had centuries of political experience behind them. The historical importance of Suez for the British people was not that they were defeated, but that they were duped. They turned from the facts to a world of pure illusion.

Illusion, indeed, is at the core of the problem of democracy as it has developed during the twentieth century in Britain and America. Self-deception is of the very air which it breathes. In foreign affairs it takes the form which Dean Acheson exposes so cruelly in his essay in the *Yale Review*.* It consists in the belief, running counter to all the realities of our situation, that there is such a thing as a world community which can be realised by incantation, and of which the full realisation is only prevented by wickedness, misunderstanding or lack of faith. This ideal world community, it is thought, is already expressed, if only in embryo, by such institutions as the United Nations and the Commonwealth, and if these are only supported to the full, the world community will grow to its proper stature, and the troubles of our proud and angry dust be stilled for ever.

But this view of the world is tragically false, and unless it is changed it will work itself out inexorably to the final cataclysm, or to the peaceful collapse of western civilisation, and a take-over by communist imperialism. For nothing is more remarkable in this world of illusion in which we increasingly have our being than the general belief that international communism is no longer a threat; that peaceful co-existence means peace; and that a European *détente* means European reconciliation. It was said of Philip of Macedon that 'peace was the first and most dangerous of his weapons of war'.† It is as true

* See page 13 above.
† André Bonnard, *Greek Civilisation from Euripides to Alexander*, p. 68.

today of world communism. Indeed the leaders of the Soviet Union, with that strange, rugged, rock-like directness which keeps breaking through the web of duplicity which is the normal expression of their policy, have never pretended that, for them, peaceful co-existence is anything more than the continuation of war by other means. And when they look upon what is happening not only in South East Asia, the Middle East and Africa but in the United States of America and the United Kingdom, they are assured that peaceful co-existence leads in the end to peaceful conquest.

The Russians may be wrong in their appraisal, but at least it is based on what they see in the world about them. The western view, by contrast, is false because the assumptions on which it is based are false. We speak of world community or of a Commonwealth. But these words imply, after all, things that are held in common— a common outlook, a common interest, a common purpose. Neither the United Nations nor the Commonwealth reflects anything of this. The United Nations is little more than an arena in which east and west, the uncommitted and the under-developed, pursue without scruple their conflicting aims. There is in fact less community of interest in the United Nations building in New York than there was in the chancelleries of Europe in the days before 1914, when the Powers, even if they pursued their separate aims, did so in the context of a civilisation which it was in their common interest to preserve.

The Commonwealth, for its part, was designed for a salve or balm to British pride and British conscience. Or if it has any reality beyond this, it is only a kind of *snobisme* which gives to the 'under-privileged' entry to the most exclusive clubs, and at the same time a most potent weapon for bringing pressure to bear upon those who propose them for membership—the threat of withdrawal. Thus, the British are subjected to a continuing process of blackmail. The idea of Commonwealth, moreover, brings in its train this additional evil, that it preserves, without the power of colonialism, all the suspicion and mistrust which colonialism inspires. It would have been very much better, when independence was given, to have cut the painter finally than to preserve this fragile web of illusion, too weak for guidance but substantial enough for misunderstanding and resentment.

People generally say of the United Nations that with all its weaknesses it is better than nothing, and certainly some of its agencies, even if they are not doing it particularly effectively, are doing work that badly needs doing, as the I.L.O., between the wars, did something to redeem the failure of the League. The United Nations, we are told, is invaluable as a safety valve, and without it political tensions in Asia and Africa would be even more evident than they already are. This, however, is only a hypothesis. What is certain is that the United Nations is a sounding board for propaganda of unparalleled efficiency and of which the purposes are essentially subversive. It used to be argued by critics of the League of Nations that its only function was to preserve the status quo. It can be said with more truth of the United Nations, that its principal function is to upset it.

The Conservative party is sometimes accused of 'paying lip service' to the United Nations. If this were so, there might be some hope, for then, perhaps, one could look forward to a Conservative government making an effort, at least, to reform the procedures in the United Nations building to bring them into some kind of relationship with the realities of the world in which it has to operate. It would be difficult to reform them, and it might prove impossible, but it is not easy to fathom the mentality of those who, fully aware of the deficiencies of the world organisation, will not even make the attempt. Or perhaps it is not so difficult after all. For the United Nations is another of the sacred cows which graze in the luscious pastures of that middle ground where the first fruits of the electoral harvest are thought to be ripening.

The attitude of the Conservative leadership towards Africa reflects illusions of the same kind. It has always been British policy to prepare colonial territories for eventual self-government, and so Mr. Iain Macleod may be forgiven for saying in 1960 that it was his purpose, as Colonial Secretary, to create in Africa parliamentary institutions on the western model. And perhaps it was natural for a government unable any longer to sustain the reality of Empire to foster the pretence that a Commonwealth, disparately composed of elements not only mutually incompatible but often actively hostile to each other, would prove an effective substitute. But how such illusions survived the experience of the next decade is more difficult to understand.

For it is evident that African society is unsuited to parliamentary government, and that the new African states, based on lines arbitrarily drawn on the map to meet the needs of colonial administration, and altogether disregarding the realities of tribal life, can only survive as

93

tyrannies, and tyrannies of a kind exceptionally cruel and harsh. I have heard it said that even if the African is more at home with dictatorship than with democracy, an African dictatorship is better than a European one. This seems to me to be a very cynical attitude. It is one of the characteristics of his temperament, as readers of the newspapers are becoming painfully aware, that the African is singularly lacking in the quality of compassion. Political independence does not necessarily have anything to do with personal freedom or even common humanity.

It is extraordinary, too, at a time when the principle of nationality is increasingly seen to be both irrelevant and dangerous, that successive British governments should have gone out of their way to create artificially new nationalities which have none of the reality and all the dangers of the old.

No one can say what the long-term effects of the scramble from Africa will be, but the complacent assumption that the new African states are only passing through the kind of teething troubles which we ourselves survived in the thirteenth or fourteenth centuries is not particularly encouraging, nor is it well founded. No doubt the continent north of the Zambezi will continue to be a running sore of instability and disaffection to be exploited endlessly by its enemies to the disadvantage of the western world. But whatever the political consequence it seems certain that the economic condition of the African people will continue to deteriorate, and the gulf between poverty and riches, between the possessing and the dispossessed to widen, unless there is a change in the attitude of the more advanced

94

societies towards the problems of the under-developed world.

There is something infinitely depressing about the argument which is interminably carried on between the political parties about which of them has made the greatest contribution to overseas aid.* For it obscures the real issue, and leads intelligent and well-intentioned people to suppose that it is simply a matter of diverting money and resources from one part of the world to another. But the problem is far more complex than that. It is not only how to make available to the under-developed world resources they lack, but also how to bring that world into the trading pattern of the developed world. This needs something more than good will or the infusion of new capital, for these things, unsupported by economic understanding, practical experience and, perhaps even more important still, some knowledge of anthropology, will not solve the problem, but only exacerbate it. It is no more possible for an ex-colonial territory than for Britain herself to thrive on a diet of doles and subsidies. In Africa, even more than in Britain, these are obstacles to economic development, because they distract attention from the reality of the problem to be solved— how to lay the foundations, scarcely existent for the most part, which are the condition of an advanced society; and how to provide the incentives which will induce men to work on these foundations rather than to sit around as they do, waiting for manna from heaven.

This does not mean that the western world can shrug

* For example, the exchange between Sir Alec Douglas-Home and Mr. Harold Wilson in the House of Commons, 30th October, 1969.

95

its shoulders and pass by on the other side. It does not mean that the under-developed world has no need of capital, or that it is not the duty of the developed world, as it is very much in its interest, to supply it. But it has the duty, too, equally important, to see to it that the new capital is applied productively. For twenty years it has been accepted that overseas aid is primarily an exercise in international charity—a fallacy which is rammed home with unceasing insistence by the leaders of the churches—and that if only the collecting boxes are filled to overflowing the problem is solved. For twenty years it has been assumed that overseas aid is a matter of government speaking unto government; that economic growth can only come through government planning, with no function for the private entrepreneur; and that instant growth can be realised by instant industrialisation. For twenty years billions of dollars have been poured into the under-developed countries, and the principal result has been that donor and recipient alike are disillusioned and embittered.

If these problems are beginning to be looked at afresh it is due less to the experience of two decades (for in this country, at any rate, governments seem to be impervious to the lessons of experience) than to the accession to the Presidency of the World Bank of a man of singular intelligence and force, Mr. Robert S. McNamara, former United States Defence Secretary. It was at his instance that a Commission was set up, headed by the former Prime Minister of Canada, Mr. Lester B. Pearson, to take a new look at the economic problems of the under-developed world. In *Partners in Development*, the Pear-

son Commission does little more than endorse the conclusions reached in McNamara's speech to the annual
meeting of the World Bank in 1968, blowing skyhigh
most of the fallacies upon which aid programmes have
been based until now.

'The preference for forced industrialisation at the
expense of farming . . . is now out of favour. Agricul-
ture has come to be regarded as desperately important,
and among other ways to raise farming output the
Pearson Report emphasises the importance of prices
. . . thus overturning an orthodoxy to which most com-
mentators, and indeed the World Bank itself, have for
too long subscribed. . . .

The Commission's endorsement of the use of prices,
its support for domestic entrepreneurship, its plea for
more private investment from abroad and indeed for
the opening of Western foreign bond markets to the
developing countries—these points taken together go
a long way towards the restoration of market mechan-
isms as the most promising means to promote economic development. This is a reversal of generally
accepted views. The fashionable consensus has at last
been shattered.'*

There is one point in particular which Mr.
McNamara stresses in his speech to the World Bank, a
point which is generally recognised, as a man recognises
an acquaintance on the far side of the street without,
however, bothering to cross the road to speak to him,

* John B. Wood, *A Critical Look At The Pearson Report,* B.B.C.
Third Programme, 30th November, 1969.

which is critical and indeed fundamental to the problem:

> 'Recent studies show the crippling effect of a high rate of population increase on economic growth on any developing country ... In terms of the gap between rich countries and poor, these studies show that *more than anything else it is the population explosion which, holding back the advancement of the poor, is blowing apart the rich and the poor, and widening the already dangerous gap between them.'*

So obsessed are we with the feelings of guilt which we have allowed to be associated with 'Colonialism' that we seem almost ready to take this sin, too, upon our shoulders.

And there is another point of crucial importance on which we must make up our minds. We have to decide whether political independence or economic development is the more important from the point of view of the peoples of the under-developed countries. We assume that they are the same things, but they can be mutually exclusive. There was a time when we thought that political independence and economic growth were opposite sides of the same coin. They are not. In these undeveloped societies, sovereign independence has itself been an obstacle to economic progress. Resources which have been made available by the developed world have been squandered on prestige projects like national airlines

---

*Robert S. McNamara, President of the World Bank for Reconstruction and Development, at the annual meeting, 30th September, 1968.

and steel rolling mills, when what was needed was education in population control and crop rotation, or the change from a subsistence to a cash economy.

It is one thing to demonstrate against apartheid or against Mr. Ian Smith's government in Rhodesia. It is another to demonstrate against economic development. It is not rational simultaneously to urge the economic advancement of the African and to distort the economy not of Rhodesia alone but of the African continent, in order to topple Mr. Ian Smith. And this is true of students and church dignitaries outside football grounds and equally true of Members of Parliament and Ministers on public platforms. One is tempted to echo the cry of Junius: 'It has pleased God to give us a Ministry and a Parliament, who are neither to be persuaded by argument nor instructed by experience.'

5

Indeed, the determination of the Conservative leadership to follow, at almost any cost, the political fashion of the day was most clearly shown by its attitude towards Rhodesia after the unilateral declaration of independence. It was perhaps right to condemn the 'rebellion', although even this is arguable. But by underwriting government policy without reserve or qualification, as though national unity in face of an external threat (which did not, of course, exist) were the prime consideration, the party leaders did more than misjudge the situation as seriously as the government itself. They

99

limited their freedom of action for the future, while, at
the same time, by creating a spurious atmosphere of
national unity, they put an effective ban on public discussion of a question which was far more open than they
ever seem to have understood.

Had it been otherwise, and had the leaders of the
opposition, while condemning the rebellion, dissociated
themselves at the start from the atmosphere of high
drama with which Mr. Harold Wilson invested it, he
would hardly have been able to persist in a policy so
damaging alike to British, African and indeed world interests. But having given their whole-hearted support to
sanctions at the outset, the opposition was unable, at a
later stage, credibly to oppose their extension by the
United Nations. And when it became clear that even
mandatory sanctions were ineffective except to unite the
Rhodesian electorate behind the *de facto* government,
while at the same time driving that government to those
very policies which it was the avowed purpose of sanctions to frustrate, the Conservative leadership did not
feel able honourably to withdraw from the position it
had taken up. Year by year the farce was re-enacted, and
the orders renewing sanctions were approved by both
Houses of Parliament. It was as though Parliament, after
the American Revolution, had solemnly re-imposed, at
the beginning of every session, like another Army Act,
the tea duties upon the American colonies.

What made the attitude of the Conservative leaders
even more extraordinary was that in everything they did
they ignored all the considerations which normally influence the Conservative mind. They committed themselves to a set of *a priori* principles which became in-

creasingly irrelevant as the situation developed not only in Rhodesia but throughout Africa. They laid down, in advance and in public, conditions for a settlement, a course of action which, as even the most junior of officials would have realised, would make any settlement impossible. And they forgot that they were dealing with their fellow-countrymen who could be relied upon to be as stubborn as they. And instead of making the best of the facts as they found them, they sought to change them, from a distance of six thousand miles and without the power to do so. Instead of doing what they could to secure the pacification of southern Africa and promote conciliation between Rhodesia and its northern neighbour, they seemed intent only to make conciliation impossible and to increase the chances of disorder.

Here again the fatal urge to stand well with 'the centre', the determination at all costs to avoid giving offence to the liberal vote, sterilised the Conservative party in opposition as it had reduced its effectiveness in government, and put limits to its freedom of action if it should ever become a government again. The price paid for the middle ground was once more a high one.

CHAPTER VI

THE CONSERVATIVE AT HOME

1

That politics is the art of the possible is a truism which begs the most important question of all: what is impossible, and what is only difficult, and how does one distinguish between them? This is a question which Conservatives, since the war, have never faced. They have assumed that the difficult must be impossible, as if by definition.

Compromise is of the essence of politics, no doubt. Indeed it is the foundation of parliamentary government, for without the capacity to concede, to give and take, majority rule would be a tyranny as harsh and ruthless here as it is in many other lands. But ultimately there are principles—or perhaps it would be truer to say that there are attitudes of mind—which cannot be seriously compromised without frustrating the very purpose of political action, the organisation of society for the safety of its members and for their well-being.

How these ends themselves are to be defined, let alone realised, is of course another matter, and each man will make his own decisions in the light of his reading of history, his experience of life and his general disposition towards hope or scepticism—according to his party allegiance, in short. But having made his decision on these very few issues the politician has an obligation to stand by it. The Socialist believes in equality and in the power of governmental action to change not only the condition but even the nature of man, by influencing his environment.* But if he is of another mind and decides that freedom is more important than equality, or that man was born in sin, a condition which no legislation can change, he is in the wrong party. In the same way, the Conservative no more believes in the possibility of equality than he believes that the moon is made of green cheese. He holds that human nature is essentially imperfect, but that men and women are most likely to make the best of it in a free society, not one which is minutely regulated from above by some agency external to themselves. He believes that his past is a part of man's nature, and that he throws tradition to the winds at his peril. And the Conservative cannot abandon these attitudes of mind, or qualify them beyond a certain point, without losing whatever usefulness he may conceive himself to have as a statesman, without losing, as they say, his credibility.

Considerations of this kind are often thought to be irrelevant when the time of Parliament and government is absorbed by economic problems, demanding for their solution not political preconceptions but objective

* 'I, as a Socialist, have had to preach as much as anyone, the enormous power of the environment as a dead destiny. We can change it; we must change it; there is absolutely no other sense in life than the work of changing it.' George Bernard Shaw, quoted in the *Times Literary Supplement*, 27th November, 1969. G.B.S. may not seem to be a serious political factor, but to think this is to misunderstand the realities of politics. It was the Fabians, of whom G.B.S. was a leading member, who created the modern Labour party.

analysis of a kind that has nothing to do with party alignments and loyalties. But quite apart from the possibility that such problems are complicated rather than simplified by the kind of analysis to which a popular assembly is likely to submit them, this thesis is untenable. One does not have to be a Marxist to know that not only the structure of society but also its quality is determined by economic decisions; and Conservative criticism of state socialism, or of the level of public expenditure exacted by the oddly-named Welfare State, is not based only on the inefficiency and economic waste engendered by them. It is founded also on the conviction that government control of industry and of the apparatus of social welfare, with the burden of taxation which accompanies it, tends to weaken the sense of responsibility of the individual citizen and stifle his initiative, and at the same time, by undermining his respect for the law and for himself, loosen the fabric of society.

2

It used to be said, in the years immediately following the last war, that the post-war readjustment had been made more smoothly and easily than after the first world war, and that there was nothing, in the late 'forties and 'fifties, comparable to the tensions and the industrial strife, verging upon revolution, which characterised the 'twenties. And this was true enough, but it was a truth which concealed a fallacy. The adjustment was easy and painless only because it was never made.

Of course it can be argued that the readjustment after the first world war was too sudden or too violent. From the beginning of time, economic history has been a record of fluctuations in prices, up or down, of greater or less intensity, relieved very rarely by brief periods of relative stability. Superimposed upon these normal fluctuations, however, there have been violent upsurges in the price level, caused by wars or other untoward events like the Black Death, the discovery of precious metals or the sudden development of new industrial techniques. Normally these abrupt and violent changes have been accepted, and economic life has proceeded after the cataclysm, whatever it may have been, from a new base line. But after 1918 the attempt was made to return to the position which had existed before the war. This proved to be impossible and the consequences were disastrous.

But it was an equal error after 1945, and may yet prove to have been a fatal one, to encourage the opposite tendency. The British economy, its over-full employment and its Welfare State, were eased gently forward on a creeping tide of inflation, with high taxation and accelerating wage demands its inevitable concomitants. Inflation, which had been engaged as servant, became the master of economic policy.

There is no need to stress, for they are sufficiently well known, the effects of inflation upon the balance of payments—prices spiralling upwards, wages rising to meet them and the costs of production rising in turn to absorb wage increases, and prices spiralling upwards again. There is momentary relief when the currency, already debased, is formally devalued. For a time we are on level terms with our competitors in overseas markets; we may even have the advantage of them; and then, because the inflationary process at home continues unchecked, we fall behind again and the disastrous cycle is renewed.

But the consequences of inflation are by no means confined to its direct economic effects. These, although the most obvious, are the least of the evils which attend it. Far more corrosive of the foundations of society is the influence of inflation upon the behaviour of individuals, and on the relationship between government and governed.

When prices are continuously rising, everyone seeks to insulate himself from the consequences, even though the effort to do so only intensifies their severity. *Sauve qui peut* is the rule, alike for the shareholder and the man on the shop floor; greed, always latent in human nature but qualified in civilised societies by a sense of mutual obligation, becomes the mainspring of action, and every man's hand is turned against his neighbour in the effort to protect himself. It is often said that we have become a crassly materialistic society. If this is so, it is because the social atmosphere which is generated by continuously rising prices is such as to bring out the less attractive side of human nature. Alexander Hamilton said that it was 'the duty of a wise government to enlist men's passions in order to make them subservient to the public good'.* The easy-going and well-intentioned financial policies of post-war governments in Britain have been based on precisely the opposite principle: they have enlisted greed and fear to undermine the public good.

When prices are continuously rising, some of the most

* Speaking in the Federal Convention, quoted by Morison and Commager, *The Growth of the American Republic,* Vol. I, p. 333.

valuable elements in society are put at a disadvantage. The professional classes, it is true, are not without a line of defence, even if it is not a very edifying one, or one that they would naturally choose: they can threaten to strike. I wonder whether there has been any other time in our history when schoolteachers, of all people, would have shown the ruthless disregard for the children in their care which is expressed by strike action.

But the middle classes in general, historically an influence making for stability and cohesion, and from which so great a contribution to learning and knowledge has come, are defenceless now. Once they could protect themselves by a close study of the financial columns of the newspapers, or by choosing a good or a lucky stockbroker. This was not necessarily what they were born to do, nor was it the way in which they could best raise the quality of their own lives or the lives of others. But even this escape hatch has been closed. There can only be a handful who have been able to defeat inflation through setting up businesses and floating them on the stockmarket. These fortunate ones could be counted by the hundred, but for the great bulk of middle-class professional people there is no escape.

And something more than injustice is at issue here, although it is clearly unjust to rob and pillage a particular section of society for no better reason than that it is easier that way. There is folly, too, for there is no surer recipe for revolution than to wipe out the middle class of society.

And the same process which changes for the worse the relations of individuals with each other begins to affect the relationship of the citizen with the state. 'Those who

108

wish to preserve freedom,' writes Professor Hayek, 'should recognise that inflation is probably the most important single factor in that vicious circle wherein one kind of government actions make more and more government control necessary.' For even a very moderate degree of inflation 'ties the hands of those responsible for policy by creating a situation in which, every time a problem arises, a little more inflation seems the only easy way out'.* The time comes when there are only two social classes, government and governed. And as there is no check on the one, so there is no protection for the other.

3

It is understandable that the post-war Labour government should have been careless of the inflationary effects of the policies that it favoured, and that the Labour government which came into office in 1964 should have intensified the inflationary process. It was not that these governments wanted inflation. Indeed, they would sooner have done without it, if only for its effect upon the balance of payments. But for them there was what seemed to be a compensating advantage to offset the disadvantages: for they cherished the illusion that inflation, by its levelling propensity, positively makes for 'social justice' and a more equal society. At least they had reasons for what they did, even if they were bad reasons. But what is less easy to understand is why successive Conservative governments, with very different social purposes, should have persisted in policies which

* Hayek, *Constitution of Liberty*, pp. 338–9.

differed only in degree, not in kind, from those of their political opponents.

When the war ended, the 'twenties and 'thirties were still close enough in time to make it seem that deflation and mass unemployment were the enemies to be feared. But by the late 'fifties, at any rate, it should have been clear that our troubles were of a very different order. And yet Mr. Harold Macmillan, Prime Minister from the beginning of 1957 until the end of 1963, can have made very few speeches on domestic policy without referring to his experiences as Member for Stockton-on-Tees during the depression of the 'thirties, and without expressing his determination to shield the British people from another such calamity. Only those who represented working-class constituencies in the north of England during the Parliament of 1931 and 1935 can understand the feelings of helplessness and despair with which Mr. Macmillan must have watched those listless groups standing on the street corners, hour after hour, day after day, month after month, human beings denied the possibility of human hope. But the fact that he could not clear his mind of these tragic memories must certainly have clouded his judgement, for the problems which he was called upon to face, twenty and twenty-five years later, were very different. Without these preconceptions he might, indeed, have regarded the resignation of a Chancellor of the Exchequer, unable to persuade his colleagues to accept cuts in public expenditure, as something more than 'a little local difficulty'—a phrase which attracted the headlines and elicited a certain kind of amused admiration, but which reflected a strange obtuseness and insensitivity to the true nature of the world about him and the forces which were moulding it.*

It is usual nowadays to argue that a degree of inflation, properly controlled, is both inevitable and desirable. There is the experience of other countries. Here the value of money has dropped from 100 in 1958 to 74 in 1968, but in the Netherlands, Italy, Portugal and Norway it fell to 72 and in France to 69. Even the United States and Germany show a fall in the value of money during the decade of 17 and 20 points respectively against our own 26 points.† We should count our blessings, therefore, and understand that we are only sharing the common experience of mankind—as indeed we shared it during the 'thirties without, however, taking much comfort from the fact. Let us not deceive ourselves. If inflation is a sickness it makes it no better that the infection is worldwide: it only makes it more difficult to correct, and more dangerous.

A gentle increase in the price level—say three or four per cent a year—makes things easier, it is said. It encourages 'growth'; it avoids the necessity for harsh decisions; above all it is perfectly respectable. It is incon-

* In the autumn of 1957, it is true, it seemed momentarily as though we might be facing something comparable to the events of 1929 and 1931. A downturn in the American economy, a partial devaluation of the franc and rumours of a general re-alignment of European currencies, resulted in a scarcely-controllable run on sterling. But as Lord Robbins pointed out in *Lloyds Bank Review* in the spring of 1958, although the crisis seemed to have been generated externally, its roots were here, and sterling would not have suffered as it did had it not been for the mismanagement of the British economy in earlier years and the inflationary pressures thus generated.

† Monthly Economic Letter of the First National City Bank of New York. September, 1969.

ceivable, it is said, that there should be a runaway inflation in this country. 'It can't happen here.' It is said that a comparison with Germany has no validity, for inflation there was the result of defeat in two wars and of political factors like the French invasion of the Ruhr after the first war and the German reaction to it, which have no application here.

It is to be wondered, however, whether those who talk so lightly of the benefits of a gentle inflation have ever stopped to consider that 'such a seemingly moderate increase in prices as three per cent per annum means that the price level will double every twenty-three and a half years and that it will nearly quadruple over the normal span of a man's working life' or to reflect upon the social and political consequences of such a progression.* As the distinguished American economist, Mr. Leon Henderson, has observed: 'A little inflation is like a little pregnancy; it keeps on growing.' To say, with positive assurance, that a persistent inflation will not be damaging, or that it can be kept at a predetermined level, is to make some very bold assumptions indeed. They are not the kind of assumptions, at any rate, upon which a Conservative government ought to base its policy.

4

The causes of inflation are diverse, no doubt, some of them unfathomable and some only mysterious. But this much at least is certain. Inflation is not an act of God. It is the result of government policy, and whether the government calls itself Labour or Conservative is

* Hayek, op. cit., p. 337.

scarcely material. The same policies produce the same results.

As much as the Socialists themselves, Conservative governments have relied upon state intervention. Instead of calling in aid the forces of the market, they have tried to suppress them and, generally speaking, to suppress them by the same expedients. Of course the Conservative party is opposed to the nationalisation of industry, and when a Conservative government comes into power it denationalises this industry or that, as its predecessor nationalised it. This ritual completed, however, and the proper genuflections having been made to the idea of a free economy, it is assumed that things should go on very much as before, and that what has come to be known as a 'mixed economy' creates a sensible, equitable and creative balance of forces. It does nothing of the kind, for it gives government a licence to interfere at will with the economy as a whole, to distort whatever natural balance may be left in it.

For the effects of state intervention are not confined to nationalisation and the direct control of industry. If they were, the problem would be manageable. Nationalisation is so obvious a nonsense that it flies its own danger signals. What is far more dangerous, because cause and effect are less clearly linked, is government intervention in general, through public expenditure and taxation, investment policies, price controls, policies of overfull employment and, of course, an incurable disposition to teach other people their business. And all these things are common to both parties. Which of us, indeed, could say offhand, of all the horrid hagiology of government by interferences and incantation—Neddies big and little,

Mini-techs and Maxi-techs, wage freezes and dividend freezes, national wages policies, pay policies, guiding lights, National Incomes Commissions, Prices and Incomes Boards and all the rest of it—which particular nostrum or specific came from which particular party?

As remarkable, in its way, as the optimism which has led successive governments to suppose against all the evidence and all experience, including their own, that wages and prices can be controlled by the written or the spoken word, or that economic growth can be created by legislation, is their obsession with 'growth' itself. It has come to be assumed, as a matter of course, that it is the duty of government, and that it is within its power, to create abundance and to ensure that every family has its refrigerator, its washing machine, its coloured television, its holiday on the Costa Brava and soon, no doubt, its trip to the moon.

But there is no reason whatever to think that any government can satisfy these expectations by legislative action. Of course, as industry takes advantage of rapidly developing techniques of manufacture, goods of all kinds become available to a widening circle. But it should be clear by now that any advances made in this country have been made in spite of, not because of government intervention. That this is so is confirmed, if it is not proved, by the experience of other countries whose governments are confined to a more passive role, and whose performance outstrips our own.

But it is not only that the policies of each government in turn have been coloured by this obsession. As Mr. Russell Lewis has pointed out, a characteristic of the past decade has been the number and the variety of the nostrums which have been adopted and discarded by successive governments, expedients of which the purpose has been to find an easy and painless path to Eldorado.*

There is the idea, for example, based on one of the hoariest of economic fallacies, that a valid distinction can be made between manufacturing industry and what are known as service industries, and that from the point of view of the balance of payments manufacturing industry is good and service industry is bad; and this in spite of the fact that nearly two-fifths of our export earnings derive from service industries, and that world trade is growing faster in services than in goods. It is this fallacy which is the origin of the Selective Employment Tax, an expedient absurd in itself but no more absurd than the nostrum devised by a Conservative government, and mercifully abandoned, the resurrection of the poll-tax in the belief that it would lead to a more economical use of labour.

And then there is the idea that British industry can only compete effectively in world markets on the basis of a technological 'break-through'. This is the reason for what Mr. Harold Wilson has described as the 'restructuring' of the government machine, and for the invention and expansion of the Ministry of Technology. We are told by Mr. Wilson that unless Europe can match American technology we, with the rest of Europe, must become an American satellite. But has Mr. Wilson ever paused to ask himself why this should be so? And has Mr.

* Russell Lewis, *An End to Growth Mania*, B.B.C. Third Programme, 25th August, 1969.

I am much in Mr. Lewis' debt for this argument and for the examples which support it, although he cannot be held responsible for all the inferences I draw from them.

Heath? Mr. Russell Lewis reminds us that Japan has relied on the importation of American techniques without
becoming an American satellite. And Japan is already
the third industrial power in the world. Or, again, there
is the British computer industry upon which the Ministry of Technology prides itself so much: it is the biggest
in Europe. But it is more important to use computers
than to make them, and Western Germany, without a
Ministry of Technology, is the biggest user.

To be sceptical of Mr. Harold Wilson's 'white hot
technological revolution' is not to belittle technical
advance. It is only to suggest that one need not pioneer a
new technology in order to take advantage of it. There is
no need, therefore, to create an elaborate and expensive
structure in order to beat the Americans at their own
game, for there are other games better suited to our aptitudes and our resources. The attempt to do so, however,
creates another unnecessary distraction for industry and
a wider field for government intervention. One may,
perhaps, entertain the modest hope that a Conservative
government, on its return to power, will sweep away the
Ministry of Technology, an institution only to be justified on the assumption that governments which are
proved incompetent, on every count, to manage their own
business are especially fitted to instruct others in theirs.

But one of the most pervasive and harmful of the
fashionable cure-alls which have influenced Labour and
Conservative governments alike has been the belief that
stagnant or under-developed economies could take off
into a dazzling empyrean of economic growth simply by
doubling the rate of capital investment, a faith which
has manifested itself in this country successively as initial

allowances, investment allowances or investment grants, according to the predilections of the government or the Chancellor of the Exchequer of the day. By degrees, however, it came to be recognised that it was the kind of capital investment, not the amount, that was important. Between 1954 and 1964 what is called the public sector industry, that is the nationalised industries, took half of the total investment and used it three times as unproductively as the private sector.* As Mr. Lewis observes, had public investment been as profitable as private investment the overall rate of growth would have been 'enough to qualify us for the economic miracle club'.

And now it seems that the importance of capital investment in general, whether it is well or ill directed, is less than had been supposed, and that even in the twentieth century machines are less important than men. 'Only about one fifth of the annual growth in the United States,' says so respected an authority as Professor Milton Friedman, 'can be attributed to the direct effects of investment in the usual sense; four fifths must be attributed to the productivity of human beings.'†

If this is so, it is unnecessary to look further for a reason for the stagnation of the British economy since the war, for its recurrent crises and setbacks, and for the steady deterioration in the quality of society. What man can do to reduce 'the productivity of human beings', and to diminish their stature—whether by lecturing them, by restricting them, by taxing them, by general interference and general discouragement—has been done by every government in turn. They have indeed laid them-

* Russell Lewis, op. cit., quoting George Polanyi.
† *Capitalism and Freedom.*

selves open to de Tocqueville's indictment: 'It would seem as if the rulers of our time sought only to use men in order to make things great.'

When we consider the outlook of the two parties upon the economic problems of the day, it is possible to discern only this difference between them: the Socialist believes in what he is doing, the Conservative does not. The Socialist believes in state intervention as a thing good in itself. His philosophy is founded on the assumption that there is some abstraction—the state, the community, society, call it what you will—superior to the individuals who compose it, and which can and ought to guide and direct them. The Conservative believes nothing of the kind. But he believes nothing else. He is like a man caught up in another man's dream, and unable to break out of it.

5

The significance of Mr. Enoch Powell for the Conservative party is not the rightness or wrongness of his views on immigration, or the soundness or otherwise of his economic theory. It consists simply in this, that he is the only leading Conservative who has made his escape from the socialist dream. That is why his Conservative colleagues are afraid of him. That is why he is the only politician in any party who can fill a hall on his own merits, without the trappings of office and without the backing of a political machine. So far from 'Powellism' being a sort of moral leprosy, as it is thought to be by the high-minded and the superficial (and how often the two go together), it is a sign that the British people are ready, if only the opportunity is given them, to face the true causes of their difficulties and to eschew the easy and ineffective pabula which for so long have been ladled out to them for their ills.

What Mr. Powell has seen is what no one else has seen, that what is needed today is not tranquillisers but surgery, the cutting away of the parasitic growths which, imperceptibly but with relentless persistence, are strangling the tree of life. And he sees that what has come to be known as the 'English Sickness' is not primarily exhaustion, greed or sloth (although these are involved) but the load of taxation which bears down on the people and saps their will, and the public expenditure, positively harmful in its effect, which distorts and stultifies the economy.

It need hardly be said that Mr. Powell is not the first politician to inveigh against high taxation, or declare that public expenditure must be controlled. These are the commonplaces of politics. But he is the first politician, on either side of the House of Commons, to mean what he says. It is now generally recognised that the weight of taxation is holding us back and pulling us down, but it is taken for granted that some device can be found which will absolve us from the necessity of harsh decisions. Only Mr. Powell understands that there is no easy and painless way out of our difficulties.

It seems, however, to be the policy of both Conservatives and Socialists to seek to resolve the problem by transferring the burden from direct to indirect taxation. This is no solution. Already indirect taxation accounts for more than half of the total revenue, and already the lowest income groups are paying far more than their fair share of taxation: * it is in fact a characteristic of the present system that it is progressive beyond the bounds of reason at one end of the scale and monstrously regressive at the other. One of many illusions to which we have fallen victim is that it is the well-off under our present system of taxation who foot the bill. They do not, and they cannot: it is too high.

But even where harsh truths of this kind are beginning to be recognised, there are still hopes that somehow, by some device or other, there may be discovered an easy and painless way out of the difficulty. If, for example, the rate of economic growth is stimulated, and if at the same time the element of extreme progression in personal tax is done away with or qualified, is it not possible that the burden can be eased even without a reduction in public expenditure? It remains the same, or may even increase slightly, but because the general income has increased the rate of taxation on particular incomes can be reduced. Everyone is happy, and no one is hurt.†
But things don't turn out like this. The government, in its eager benevolence, has already discounted the expected economic growth.‡ Inflationary pressures are in-

* Colin Clark, *Taxmanship*, Hobart Paper, no. 26.
† Bryan Reading, *Buoyancy of Taxes on Income* (C.P.C.), is an excellent example of this hopeful tendency. Taxes can be reduced because incomes have increased. Another example can be found in the Conservative Central Office pamphlet *Better Times*, p. 10. 'There is one simple way of cutting taxes. It is to increase savings.' But there is no simple way of reducing taxes, and it is disheartening to find that the leaders of the Conservative party suppose that there is.
‡ Bryan Reading: *Buoyancy of Taxes on Income*. The textbook case is the treatment of the Robbins Report on Higher Education by Sir Alec Douglas-Home's government towards the end of its period of office. The recommendations of the Robbins

tensified, and if the burden seems to be eased it is only because the monetary terms in which it is expressed have been devalued. The blunt truth is that if we have decided that the weight of taxation is too heavy, or the aggregate demand upon the resources of the economy too great, there is no effective remedy other than cuts in public expenditure.*

While everyone admits the desirability of cutting government expenditure, no one believes that it is possible, and the most that is even hoped for is that expenditure should be contained at somewhere about its existing level. In this atmosphere of wary fatalism, where nothing is possible, it is hardly surprising that even this modest goal is never achieved. But before we accept so defeatist a point of view, let us ask ourselves one simple question. In the ten years from 1959 to 1968 public expenditure on current account (leaving out Defence and Local Authority expenditure) rose from £4,647 million

---

Committee involved an expenditure of more than £3 thousand million in the ten-year period, and the doubling of the annual rate of expenditure on higher education during that time. The Report was published on 23rd October, 1963, and it was accepted by the government on 24th October. Apart from the fact that there was a general election in prospect and that higher education, other things being equal, is something that is desirable in itself, the justification for this extraordinary display of irresponsibility was simply that 'economic growth' would take care of the massive additional public expenditure.

* It can be argued that there are countries which, taking taxation and social service contributions together, carry a greater burden and yet outstrip the United Kingdom in economic performance. But these are countries which do not share our economic problems and whose dependance on international trade is not, as ours is, absolute. And they are countries where, by tradition, the state has always been more important than the individual, societies upon which we would not normally wish to model ourselves.

121

to £10,074 million. It more than doubled in a decade. Granted that much of this increase was due to the inflationary pressures generated by the increase itself, the rise in expenditure was still fantastically high. The question we should ask ourselves is this: was there anything that happened in the economic and social field during these periods which made it imperative, as distinct from its being only desirable, to increase expenditure at this rate?

If the answer is that there was no overwhelming and imperative need—and it is difficult to see what other answer there can be—then it is clear that there is no overwhelming and imperative need to maintain it at that level, and that the considerations which prevent cuts being made are not economic, but political. When a politician says that it is impossible for him to make cuts, he means only that he cannot make them without losing votes. He means that it is 'politically impossible'.

But he may be wrong. There is no easy answer to the problems raised by continuously rising public expenditure, and there is no painless answer. And certainly no road will open up unless first we cut through a jungle of established habits of thought. In a speech at Morecambe Bay, in October, 1968, Mr. Powell outlined in considerable detail proposals for relieving the Budget of £2,855 million, and this without touching Defence, without touching Education, without touching Pensions or Health Services or social services of any kind. Such a relief would allow of a reduction of the standard rate of income tax to 4/3d. in the £, the halving of surtax and the abolition of the Selective Employment Tax. It is easy to see how such a reduction in the burden of taxation would transform the economic position of this country and the lives of its people.

It is easy, too, to cry 'Impossible.'* And yet the 'Morecambe Budget' is not a conjuring trick, some sleight of hand or figures, a sort of Irish Sea Bubble. It relies upon a device which, startlingly novel to our eyes, is well tried and has been the principal impulse to bring man from the Stone Age to the Space Age. It is simply this, that economic decisions should be taken on economic grounds. It is not generally realised what a very high proportion of government expenditure is devoted, not to providing services for the citizen or to defending him or to keeping him in order, but to doing things which would be done better and less expensively if they were left to the market; perhaps as much as a third of the national expenditure is thus dispersed.

Thus Mr. Powell would stop governments making payments at the taxpayer's expense, the purpose of which is 'to ensure that effort and capital are put to less profitable use than they would otherwise be'; and he would stop 'payments which are directed towards making firms and people take different decisions from those which they would otherwise take'. If this device were extended to cover the whole field of government interference with industry, it would be possible to realise Mr. Powell's aim of a tax relief of nearly £3,000 million, not at the expense of economic growth but so as to stimulate it.

Whenever it is suggested that market forces and a

* And of course the cry has been raised on every side, and pundits of every political complexion have joined in it. But see Enoch Powell, *Income Tax at 4/3 in the £*, Tom Stacey Books.

spontaneous order are more effective as a stimulus to economic activity than the slow-moving, ponderous and insensitive machinery of government, the spectre of Victorian industrialism is brought gibbering on to the stage like Sweeney's ghost. It is one of the strangest oddities of political life in this country that those who talk most fervently about bringing us into the twentieth century —or is it the twenty-first that they speak of now?—seem to spend so many of their leisure hours in the nineteenth. Unable to realise that the problems of the nineteen-seventies are not those of the eighteen-seventies they cannot understand that the problem today is not how to redistribute wealth. It is not even how to create wealth. It is how to stop governments from hindering or preventing the creation of wealth. It is arguable, even if the argument cannot be sustained (as I shall hope to show in the next section of this essay), that the central government can best organise the social services and act in general as a kind of overlord of public relief. But what has surely been proved by now is that government, itself unable to exploit the new technical revolution, can effectively prevent its exploitation by others.

All of this seems to be beyond the grasp of the leaders of the Conservative party. They inveigh against nationalisation and government control; they praise the merits of individual effort and free enterprise; but they seem to have no very clear idea of the reasons for condemning the one or extolling the other. At any rate there is no indication that they have grasped the true cause of our economic and, to a great extent of our social troubles—the clumsy and inexpert hand of government taking hold of the complex and delicate levers which actuate an industrial economy. There is evidence, indeed, that the Conservative leadership conceives of itself as being committed not to change existing policies but only to execute them more efficiently.

'With the co-operation of the Chairmen of a number of large companies,' writes the Political Correspondent of the *Daily Telegraph*, 'Mr. Heath has arranged that the next Conservative government will have at its disposal the managerial skills of fifteen to twenty senior executives now working in private enterprise. . . . Some of these are already helping the Shadow Cabinet to pinpoint problems in such areas as aircraft procurement, public building and the administration of the social services, in which management techniques adapted from private enterprise might promote "cost effectiveness". . . . When the Labour government took office in 1964 it also enlisted for government departments, such as the now defunct Department of Economic Affairs, men from private enterprise whose goodwill must have been sought beforehand.'*

Plus ça change. . . .

6

The continuing crisis through which we have lived for the past twenty-five years covers the whole spectrum of national life, political, economic, social and moral. But it is a constitutional crisis, too. By imposing upon Parliament burdens which it was never designed to bear

* *Daily Telegraph*, 17th November, 1969. See also 'We will set up under the Prime Minister a small central administration unit to ensure that the latest management techniques are introduced throughout the public sector.' Conservative pamphlet, *Better Times*.

and which, from its nature, it is quite unfitted to carry, the value of parliamentary government itself is called in question, and the foundations of a free society are threatened. 'The tendency to dictatorship in the modern world,' says Lord Robbins, 'is an inevitable result of the fact that if democratic bodies attempt to go outside a certain sphere, either they do the business inefficiently or they abdicate their functions.'*

This is an ineluctable truth from which, by some mental blockage, Conservatives seem to have cut themselves off. They take it for granted that there is nothing to be done or, less understandably, that there is nothing that needs doing. Even so respected a Conservative as Lord Brooke of Cumnor, reflecting upon the high quality of the membership of the House of Commons, asks himself this question: 'But will enough of such men and women be willing to face ... the frustrations of a member's life, as the years go on *and as Parliament keeps getting busier?*'† But why this fatalism? Why does Lord Brooke take it for granted that the House of Commons must take on more and more work until the end of recorded time? Why should the load not be lightened? Why does Lord Brooke assume that from decade to decade the freedom of the individual will be restricted still further, and the power of government over him still further increased? And in what essential respect, one wonders, does he distinguish between the society that he foresees and any other socialist society?

But this is not the worst of it. By struggling ineffectively to force Parliament to do what it was never de-

* Lionel Robbins, *The Great Depression*, p. 193.
† An article in *The Times*, 25th April, 1966 (my italics).

signed to do, and what it is incapable of doing, modern governments, Labour and Conservative alike, have had neither time nor energy nor interest left for those tasks which governments alone can do. They have been so busy developing new technologies or hampering their development, that they have never stopped to consider the effects of modern technology on the human environment. The most minute regulations are promulgated and enforced concerning the temperature of business offices, the hours during which a box of chocolates may be sold, or the precise siting, and colour, of a notice board erected in a suburban garden, but there is no such particularity about the rules governing the disposal of industrial waste.

This is not a question, as it is sometimes thought to be, of amenity. The pollution of rivers is not something that affects only the angler. The oil that is washed up on our beaches is not just a matter for the holiday maker and the local shopkeeper seeking his custom. These are things that affect the balance of nature and the future of life itself. Here is one example. Rear-Admiral Sir Edmund Irving, formerly Hydrographer of the Royal Navy, tells us that sea life is disappearing because of the vast amount of chemicals poured into the sea by every industrial nation. 'Unless pollution is stopped we will have in our lifetime a vivid example before us of the result. We will be surrounded by dead seas.'*

* *Daily Telegraph,* 19th January, 1970. But for a full study of this problem see Lynette Hamblin *Pollution: The World Crisis,* Tom Stacey Books. It must be added that the Conservative party was aware of these problems before it became fashionable to be aware of them. See David Price, M.P., *Science and Technology,* C.P.C. Outline Series No. 5. 1968.

Problems of this kind may be insoluble and it may be that we have already pronounced our own doom. But at least they could have been foreseen. And yet governments, priding themselves on their ability to plan the economy, have never asked themselves the simple and obvious question: what is to be done with waste that is deadly poisonous, that does not disintegrate with time and cannot be destroyed by any agent so far available? If this question cannot be answered by governments, because they are too busy doing what they are unfitted to do and what can be better done by others, there is no one else who will answer it.

For it is natural that engineers and chemists should overlook or discount any disadvantage which may result from their well-intentioned labours. There is no reason to expect industrialists, continuously reproached by politicians and journalists for being too cautious in adopting new techniques, to guard against the long-term effects which may result from their use, or even to be aware of them. Nor can a farmer who accepts a drainage grant from a benevolent Ministry be held responsible for the flood that ensues, perhaps a hundred miles away, because he has drained his land. These are responsibilities that can only be discharged by government. One of the most powerful arguments for dismantling the omnicompetent state is that government would be free to do those things which must be done, which only government can do, and which are not being done now.

CHAPTER VII

THE HOAX OF THE WELFARE STATE

1

In their attitude toward the Welfare State, as it was set up immediately after the war, Conservative leaders accepted quite uncritically the measures of the Attlee government. They had no choice. Here, at any rate, sustained opposition would have been in very truth 'politically impossible'. The Conservative party, moreover, was already committed by its membership of the wartime coalition to the cradle-to-grave conception of state welfare, and the experience of the inter-war years, still very recent, would in any case have deterred it from resisting proposals designed to prevent a return to the social conditions of the 'thirties.

But the Welfare State, as it was conceived during and after the war, was based on certain assumptions which seemed to be valid then but which are more questionable today. These were both practical and theoretical. It was taken for granted that, for the greater part of the population, there could be no welfare services unless they were provided by the state. This, no doubt, is what was in Mr. Aneurin Bevan's mind when he told the Labour Party Conference in 1945: 'If we were rich enough we would not want to have free medical services; we would pay the doctors.'

And what was true of the health services seemed to be

equally true of education, housing and everything else. We were living then with a low-wage economy and in a society in which, it was thought, there would be periods of depression and unemployment even if every effort were made to avoid or shorten them. No one foresaw a world in which every factory would have to provide parking space for its employees' motor cars, and holidays abroad would be a commonplace for every class except the very poorest.

In the twenty-five years following the second world war a great deal happened, then, to call in question the practical assumptions upon which the Welfare State was based. First, there was an increase in the living standards of the British people remarkable by any test. Between 1958 and 1968 income from employment and self-employment increased from £15,000 million to £28,000 million.* Of course, much of this increase is illusory and the result of inflation, itself a consequence of mistaken policies. Even so, the real increase after taking account of increased prices, is 38 per cent.

Second, and in spite of this very considerable advance in real incomes, public expenditure on the social services doubled between 1960/61 and 1968/9, and the proportion spent on them rose from 15 per cent to 20 per cent of the national output.

Third, despite the increase in real incomes and the doubling of social expenditure, *we are not spending enough on the relief of poverty*. The benefits accruing from this vast expenditure, so far from being too high, are too low 'in relation to the needs of people who either have exceptionally low incomes apart from state help

* *National Income and Expenditure*, 1969, H.M.S.O., Table 19.

(mainly the old) or else exceptionally heavy claims on a modest income (mainly large families among low wage earners).'*

The conjunction of these three factors—the increase in personal incomes, the increase in social expenditure and the increase in poverty—must surely indicate that there is something seriously wrong with the organisation of the Welfare State. One of the conclusions that can certainly be drawn is that a very high proportion of social expenditure by government and local authorities, as much, perhaps, as two-thirds of it, goes to families whose tax payments equal or exceed the value of the benefits they receive: supposing they themselves to be the beneficiaries of the Welfare State, they are in fact its milch-cow.†

Long after it had become apparent that the Welfare State was a cruel hoax, that it did little or nothing to relieve poverty and that its effect, so far as the great mass of the population was concerned, was to take away more in taxation and contributions than it gave in 'benefits', the leaders of the Conservative party seemed to be incapable of standing back and re-examining the principles on which social provision by the state is based. In this field, as in so many others, they were the slaves of fashion, afraid of the electoral consequences of breaking away from it and more concerned to follow opinion than to influence it.

It is true that there are signs of a change today. There is much talk about 'selectivity' in the social services, and about giving help where it is most needed. This com-

* *Policy for Poverty*—Editor, Arthur Seldon. Research Monograph 20, p. 13.
† Ibid, pp. 27–32 and pp. 60–61.

mands general assent, but it is too ambiguous to mean very much without some more precise definition. It may mean that, because living standards have risen so markedly over the past twenty years, a great part of the population can safely be removed from the field of state provision and given the opportunity of making provision of their own. Or it may mean no more than that any future increase in benefits will be concentrated on those most in need. In the one case there is room for substantial reductions in public expenditure and, as a corollary, decreases in taxation real enough to create new incentives, without at the same time increasing inflationary pressures. In the other, it is the mixture as before, the dose to be increased as the general election approaches. No one can say which it will be. But the auguries are not favourable.

Speaking in the House of Commons some weeks after the devaluation of sterling in 1967, Mr. Harold Wilson claimed that the government over which he had presided for three years had increased government expenditure on social security by 48 per cent, on education by 42 per cent, on health and welfare by 45 per cent, and that local authority expenditure had increased by 46 per cent, all of these increases at constant prices. If this was intended as a defence against the charge of mismanagement of the economy, it was a very odd one. It was odd, too, that the Conservative opposition had voted against none of these increases when they came before the House of Commons. But what was even odder was Mr. Heath's speech, when he wound up the Conservative Party Conference at Brighton two years later. He suggested that Mr. Wilson's claim thus to have increased expenditure on the social services did not give a true picture of the facts: the last Conservative government, Mr. Heath said, was increasing welfare expenditure, at the end of its term of office, at a rate even higher than that which Mr. Harold Wilson had been able to achieve.*

It is hardly surprising that the Conservative party's vaunted ability to finance reductions in taxation through equivalent reductions in expenditure is sometimes thought to be suspect. There are times when words speak just as loudly as actions, but perhaps not quite so clearly.

2

But the Welfare State, as at present conceived, is founded on two other principles, neither of them based on experience and each derived from purely *a priori* conceptions of what constitutes social justice. The first is that state help must always be universal and that it must always be equal; the second, which follows from it, is that private provision for welfare is bad in itself because it must be unequal. Both of these propositions have now been demolished, not by Mr. Heath or Mr. MacLeod, but by Mr. Richard Crossman, the most eminent as he is the most doctrinaire of the Socialist intellectual establishment. In the White Paper on *National Superannuation and Social Insurance* (Cmnd. 3883. H.M.S.O. 1969) laid before Parliament by the Secretary of State for

* 'Allowing for all the price rises, the increases in social service spending in our last four years was actually faster than in the last four years under Labour.' Brighton, October, 1969. Compare St. Albans, January, 1970, where Mr. Heath 'also attacked government spending which, he said, had doubled in five years'. *Daily Telegraph,* 28th January, 1970.

Social Services, Mr. Crossman says that 'the existing flat-rate scheme of pensions' (that is, equal pensions for all) 'has failed', and that the whole scheme must be reconstructed. And he goes on to make an admission which gives away the whole case for universality and equality.

'People are prepared to subscribe more,' says Mr. Crossman, '. . . for their own personal or family security than they would ever be willing to pay in taxation.' What Mr. Crossman is saying here is not only that human beings are apt to put their own interests before those of others, and are entitled so to do, but also that in one field at least, that of superannuation and pensions, the conditions are already beginning to operate which Mr. Aneurin Bevan indicated would make this kind of provision unnecessary.[*]

But Mr. Crossman goes a long way further than this. In his Herbert Morrison Memorial Lecture *Paying for the Social Services*,[†] he has this (with much else) to say:

> 'Up to the end of the 1920's Disraeli's two nation concept held good. The British people were divided into a privileged minority enjoying a high standard of living and economic security, and at the other end a majority who were poor or only just above that level and expected to remain so. During the period since I became an active Socialist, Britain has been transformed into a community where the majority are affluent and only a minority are poor.'

This being so evidently the case, is it reasonable to continue to organise the social services as if it were not?

[*] See page 129 above.
[†] Fabian Tract, No. 399.

But let Mr. Crossman proceed:

'The housewife whose domestic gadgets provide the equivalent of four maids' work, and the husband whose car puts him on the level with the owner of a coach and four (not to mention the coachman) already feel in their own lives that material living standards which were once the privilege of a small property owning class are being transformed into the legitimate expectations of every reasonably industrious citizen. Very soon, the ever increasing expectations extend from physical goods and material well-being to such concepts as health, education and security in old age.'

And why in the world not?

But why insist on everything being paid for by the very clumsy, and in economic terms extremely wasteful, combination of taxation and what Mr. Crossman elegantly describes as 'claw-back'—that is, giving benefits to everyone and then withdrawing them from the majority by taxation, operating through a means test? For this is an expedient of which the only conceivable purpose is to maintain, at any cost in terms of inconvenience to the citizen and expense to the taxpayer, a purely theoretical principle of equality.

This principle of the claw-back is illustrated, in all its waste and folly, by what happned to Family Allowances between July, 1967, and January, 1968. In 1967 it was decided, very properly, that 160,000 families needed an increase in family allowances. To preserve the sacred principle of equality it was necessary to pay an extra seven shillings a week to four million families—of whom three million eight hundred and forty thousand did not need it. The cost was £120 million, but of this £30 million was recovered by the normal operation of income tax, reducing the net cost to £90 million.

In January, 1968, however, it became necessary because of devaluation to make still further cuts. But again these had to be made without weakening the principle of equality. Accordingly, income tax allowance for children was reduced, thus bringing the cost of the increased family allowances down from £90 million to £30 million.

It has been estimated that if an outright payment had been made to the 160,000 families who needed increased family allowances, without any of the rigmarole of taxation and claw-back, the direct cost would not have been £120 million, or £90 million, or £30 million, but £13 million; and this with the added advantage that all those in need would have benefited instead of only a proportion of them, and that a considerable administrative cost would have been saved.*

In a moving passage in this same lecture, Mr. Crossman describes an occasion when he was entertained to luncheon by the late Lord Marks, Chairman of Marks and Spencer. He was deeply impressed in particular by the excellence of the fruit salad, a memory which has haunted him for twenty years. But one must have the story in his own words:

'Having been presented with a particularly delicious and exotic fruit salad, I couldn't resist remarking on it to the Chairman of Marks & Spencer. He

* *Policy for Poverty*, op. cit., p. 24.

looked at me with those huge gentle brown eyes and observed with great seriousness, "That fruit salad you ate was not only good but extremely expensive. It is the aim of this organisation, my dear Dick, within the next ten years to make it possible for the average citizen to eat that fruit salad at Marks & Spencer. Life for me consists of noticing what is really worth having among the pleasures of the rich and enabling everyone to get them." What Sir Simon said was not only relevant to his own firm, it expresses a truth about the technological revolution in which we live. With each succeeding decade what were once the exclusive luxuries of the rich become available for cash at a price which the average citizen can pay.'

This is certainly an edifying and improving tale, but there are two points arising from it upon which, if he has noticed them, Mr. Crossman does not pause to reflect. The first is this. While the firm of Marks & Spencer has brought within the reach of people of moderate means a wide range of goods of a quality hitherto denied to them, it has done this as a marketing operation, conducted for profit; it is in the highest degree unlikely, to say the least of it, that a nationalised industry would have produced the same result. The second thing to notice is what has happened, since the day when he first tested this particularly exotic and delicious fruit salad, to the price of Marks and Spencer shares. £100 invested in Marks & Spencer 'A' shares in 1949 was worth £1,631 in 1969. This means that the shareholders of Marks & Spencer are in a position, through no merit of their own, to consume very much more delicious and exotic fruit salad than

137

others. Were the problem presented to him in these terms Mr. Crossman, no doubt, would sooner have us all do without fruit salad.

And there is no reason except this doctrinaire insistence on an unattainable equality why the principle that applies to Mr. Crossman's exotic dessert should not apply equally to health, housing or education. It is only that the idea is novel that it seems at first to be chimerical. There is a kind of inertia built into the human brain, something quite distinct from the conservative instinct, which prevents even the most progressive minds from re-examining their own preconceptions.

The idea that education, for instance, should be paid for by the parent, wholly or in part, is neither novel nor old-fashioned; it is commonplace. I remember, when I led a parliamentary delegation to the Soviet Union some years ago, being told by Mr. Richard Crossman's equivalent, a man perhaps a little less doctrinaire than he, that the Soviet authorities did not believe that the citizen should have anything for nothing, and that even the mother who left her infant in a crêche when she entered the factory must make some payment towards the cost.

In Australia, to go to another hemisphere and another world, there is no universal national health service as we understand it. The Australian insures himself against sickness and the need for hospital treatment. He pays his doctor. He pays a fee for his medical prescription which makes our own prescription charges look something less than minimal. And although education is free, the parent is still obliged to pay for school books, and the parents' associations for any extra amenities that the schools may enjoy. And with it all one can fairly say that

Australian society is not grossly 'unequal', or that there is more poverty in Australia than here: in fact there is a good deal less. There is, too, in Australia an artistic and literary explosion, more real if less pretentious than anything that is happening here. And what can also be said is that the Australian citizen, of any class, retains an independence of character which in this country we seem determined to suppress.*

It is natural for Mr. Crossman to insist on equality (whether one calls it 'equality' or 'equality of opportunity' really matters very little) but it is difficult to see why Conservatives should blindly follow him. For this there are, I think, two explanations. In the first place equality is good or is thought to be good business, electorally speaking; *a fortiori*, inequality must be very bad business. Secondly, Conservatives have never bothered to make the intellectual effort necessary to test propositions of which the truth seems to be self-evident.

Mr. Aneurin Bevan, when he introduced the National Health Service, said that its purpose was 'to generalize the best'. This, of course, was a meaningless statement, and what Mr. Bevan intended to convey, no doubt, was that the suppression or discouragement of private practice, by spreading the butter more widely but more thinly, would raise the level of the average. But this is not how, in any field, the average is raised. It is raised by the gradual dissemination of exceptional excellence. It is raised, in short, by precisely that inequality which Mr. Crossman condemns and which the leaders of the Conservative party, for different, more practical and possibly

---

* In Australia the social services vary from state to state, but nowhere can one find anything resembling the British system.

less admirable reasons, equally deplore.* The attempt to generalise the best has had the effect of lowering the average, not raising it, for as Mr. Freeman points out in the letter quoted below, it has resulted, *inter alia*, in the permanent emigration from this country of twenty per cent of the doctors trained here, and their replacement by doctors trained in poorer countries, which have an even greater need of them than we have. 'Mr. Crossman's is a policy of short-term fairness,' Mr. Freeman continues, 'leading to no long-term gain (save possibly, for him, in the electoral sense).'

In the field of education too, there is the same kind of intellectual confusion, and the Conservative leadership repeats the prevailing shibboleths without debate of any kind. Whether it is a matter of the number of graduates in this country compared with other countries, or of the 'neighbourhood effects' of education, or the raising of the school leaving age, or the value of the public school system, certain assumptions are accepted and acted upon,

* The point is put with moderation and much force by Mr. M. A. R. Freeman, Consultant Orthopaedic Surgeon to the London Hospital, in a letter to *The Times*, 8th December, 1969. In Mr. Freeman's view 'the moral axiom that every member of a community has a natural right to equal standards of medical care at a given moment in time ... is not in fact in the long-term interests of the community. So expensive has modern medical care become that no society is able to afford universal excellence. Excellence must either be absent or confined to a limited number of centres. The advances in the standards of medical care which have occurred in the last century have usually been introduced in centres of excellence and have only subsequently been made available.... This fact is in conflict with Mr. Crossman's presumed axiom. It has however resulted in a steady advance in the standards of medical care, as a consequence of which the under-privileged of today are receiving care equal to that of the privileged of yesterday.' It is Mr. Crossman's fruit salad served in a slightly different way.

not because they have been proved by experience or because they can be justified by reason, but simply because it has never occurred to 'responsible politicians' to question them.

It is taken for granted that a degree in cosmetics at some obscure American college is equal to a degree at Oxbridge in chemistry, or that a graduate 'mortician' is equal to a graduate physicist. Numbers are all. It is forgotten that an apprentice steel worker in South Wales, or an apprentice shipwright on the Clyde, whose father and grandfather and great-grandfather were steelworkers or shipwrights before him, has an ingrained technical aptitude which is by no means to be despised, and which gives him a marked advantage over his American or Russian counterpart. It is taken for granted, by Lord Robbins and others, and accepted quite uncritically by the public at large, that education *per se* has secondary but beneficial effects upon the population as a whole, because it discourages crime, creating a better-informed electorate and producing 'more culturally alive neighbourhoods'. None of this has been proved, and most of it would seem to be disproved by experience.*

Again, it is accepted without question that it must be to the public advantage to raise the school leaving age from fifteen to sixteen. To let things continue as they are so that young people who feel, or whose parents feel, that it would be in their interest to stay on at school beyond the existing school leaving age are free to do so (as in fact they are doing in increasing numbers) is thought to be inadmissible. The fact that classes are already too big, that teachers are too few and ill-paid, that the rate of

* E. G. West, *Education and the State*, pp. 32–3.

141

juvenile delinquency is already highest among those who are compelled to stay at school against their inclination, that schools are not the only conceivable purveyors of education, and that the home, the factory and life itself count for something as educational influences—all of these considerations are brushed aside.* It is easy to understand why they have little effect upon the minds of those whose cardinal belief is that government can effectively replace the parent, and the local authority the family. It is more difficult to see why those who profess their faith in the family and in the responsibility of the parent for its welfare should do no more than echo the prevailing view.

And those Conservatives who believe in the merits of the public school system seem very often to harbour feelings of the deepest guilt. A public school education, they are told, promotes 'social divisiveness' and reaffirms privilege. By attracting to itself the best teachers, it impoverishes the state education system (another sample of the old fallacy that you improve the average by destroying the best). Above all, and worst of all, the public school has the capacity to produce a class of leaders, fitted to accept responsibility and even perhaps, to exercise authority. A democratic society does not need leaders, we are told: what it needs is government, and the more of it the better.

Again, it is easy to understand why arguments of this kind should carry weight with Mr. Harold Wilson or Mr. Edward Short, for whom equality is the highest good and 'the smack of firm government' the most pleasant of

* Ibid., pp. 36–9, 87–91. Dr. West's book is a most valuable corrective to fashionable educational concepts.

music. But unless one believes that there should only be two classes in society, government and governed, there is no need to be influenced by them or to believe that that society is best which, because it is without leaders of its own, is most at the mercy of the state. The public school as we know it today was founded by Arnold of Rugby to give to the new ruling class which was emerging from the industrial revolution a sense of responsibility and purpose. Today another ruling class is coming forward, born of a technical revolution. There is evidence enough to indicate that it, too, would be the better for a sense of responsibility and purpose. The English public school system was not designed to teach young Englishmen to rule colonial peoples, but to teach them to rule themselves. Conservatives should ponder deeply before they abolish an institution which has served their country so well, or let it die of inanition. Instead of limiting and confining it, they should seek rather to extend it.

3

If it is indeed the case, as most certainly it would seem to be, that the majority of people are having things done for them which they would be perfectly well able to do for themselves were it not for the burden of taxation which weighs them down, while a minority are deprived of the help that they need, the problem is clearly capable of solution. Indeed, there is one solution which has been much canvassed, in this country and more particularly in the United States, and which, leaving aside for the time being any administrative or other difficulties attending it, seems to provide an answer as complete as any that is likely to be found in an imperfect world.

It is simply this. Let that majority which is in a position to pay for, or contribute towards, the education of its children; to pay for its medical care; to pay for the roof over its head, and to pay for its own superannuation, do just these things, and let it be relieved of the tribute which the government exacts in order to do, on its behalf, the same things but at a greater cost, with less variety and with less efficiency. At the same time let the minority, the old, the disabled and the lower-paid worker, who cannot afford, no matter to what extent they are relieved of taxation, to buy these things, be provided not with the services themselves but with the means to pay for them.

This is the system, of which there is more than one form, known as Reverse Income Tax (R.I.T.), and its surpassing merit is not that it makes for equality but for inequality, and that it uses inequality for the public good. For if the majority is relieved of the heavy burden of taxation, and thus put in a position to pay for its own doctor, its own house, its own pension and the education of its own children, it becomes relatively easy to relieve the poverty of the minority, and to do so without all the cumbrous, expensive and inefficient machinery of over-generous benefits qualified by the claw-back system which still fails to get rid of poverty. Let us look, then, in more detail at the workings of R.I.T. and the problems raised by it.

It has been calculated that a family of two adults and two children 'break even' (that is to say that the benefits they receive equal what they pay by contribution or taxation) at an income of £900; that two-thirds of the households in the United Kingdom have incomes above £1,000 and that their share of *social security benefits in cash* amounts to one-third of the total. On this basis, the value of *cash* benefits received is about £1,000 million for 1968/69. The value of the National Health services received by households with an income of more than £1,000 per annum (that is, households that are now paying more in taxation than they are receiving in benefit) is estimated at £900 million.

If, then, the two are added together, social security benefits in cash and National Health service costs, there is scope for a remission of taxation of the order of £1,900 million. Because of the substitution of Reverse Income Tax payments for the present cash payments to families with lowest incomes, that is incomes below the break-even point, there would be an additional expenditure of £100 million. This would be the extra tax requirement to offset the saving of public expenditure arising from the removal of people with higher incomes from this part of the state welfare system. The net remission in taxation would be, therefore, £1,900 million less £100 million, that is £1,800 million.

But relief of this kind is by no means the only benefit to be derived from Reverse Income Tax. Not only are the disincentive effects of excessive taxation removed. New incentives are created which do not exist today. A man will work harder, enjoy his work more and be a more responsible citizen, if he is able thereby to give his children a better education, or secure preferential treatment for his wife if she is in need of a major operation. No longer does he balance in his mind the advantage or disadvantage of drawing unemployment pay, combined

K   145 with a rebate of income tax, against the prospect of over-time and a differential rate of tax. For nothing could be more misleading than to imagine that it is in the higher income groups alone that taxation acts as a disincentive.* And it is sheer self-delusion to suppose that some-one who shuffles off his responsibilities on to the community, or the state, is for that reason a better citizen than the man who shoulders his own.

Another advantage is the simplification of the tax system which results from R.I.T. It is now generally recognised that the present system of tax collection, elaborated through generations of misplaced ingenuity, and of which a disproportionate part is to detect and prevent tax evasion, is in danger of a total breakdown. It is recognised, too, that too much of the time, brains and energy of those who work in industry, whether in the boardroom or on the shop floor, is devoted to the search for methods of avoiding imposts which are thought to be unfair or which militate against efficiency. Most of these troubles would disappear, or be greatly diminished under R.I.T.

At the same time there would be a contraction, if not the elimination of the elaborate machinery for the provision of social security benefits, of which the means test is a cardinal feature today. There would be no test of means other than an extension down the income scale of that now embodied in the ordinary income tax return. Nor would there be any need of special machinery for the payment of the cash subsidies which, under R.I.T.,

---

* As to the higher income groups, the cost of reducing surtax so that the top rate payable on earned income would be no more than 14/9d. in the £ would be £4 million out of total public spending of £20,000 million. *Hansard,* 9th March, 1967.

would replace all existing social security payments. Indeed the Revenue would be relieved in large measure of complexities and drudgeries against which it struggles today with increasing desperation and diminishing effectiveness.*

But if there are clear advantages to be gained from R.I.T., there are difficulties, some of them formidable, which have to be faced. If the parent is free to choose for himself his children's school, it will still be necessary to ensure that the child gets an education up to a certain standard. It will be necessary, too, to lay down a minimum standard of insurance for superannuation or medical care, on the analogy of the requirement that motorists insure against third party risks. And there are other administrative problems to which, however complicated they may be, ingenuity can be expected to provide a solution: it is forgotten today that P.A.Y.E. was long and strenuously resisted by the Revenue, on the grounds that it was unworkable.

There is one problem, however, to which there is no complete solution. In any R.I.T. scheme which aims to end poverty once and for all, there remains a weakness. If government explicitly undertakes to make family income up to a minimum level, those assisted will have a smaller inducement to exert themselves to the point where they become self-reliant. In other words, there is the danger of extending 'pauperisation' by undermining the individual's determination to increase by his own

---

* There have been indications that the Conservative party intends to recast the taxation system through the value-added tax. Whatever the merits of this tax may be, it can only, one would have thought, put an intolerable burden on the tax-gatherer.

147

effort an inadequate income which 'the state' will automatically supplement.

But no charge of pauperisation can lie in the case of pensioners or the handicapped, since, if their incomes are low or non-existent, any policy that is intended to do away with poverty must make them dependent on public subsidies of one kind or another. For others, those within whose powers it is to earn all or most of the income necessary to maintain their families above the poverty line, a system of R.I.T. would require applicants to accept suitable work, or produce bona fide evidence of their incapacity, as a qualification for benefit in cash or voucher form. Only for the most incurably work-shy, therefore, would such a radical policy to end poverty justify the charge of pauperisation. And even this minority must be expected to diminish as rising real incomes from active employment in a vigorous free enterprise economy increase the penalties of idleness on a subsistence payment under R.I.T.

4

At first sight proposals of this kind must seem far-fetched, over-elaborate and too radical in their nature to warrant serious consideration. But the alternative course of permitting existing tendencies, ever accelerating, to continue unchecked is worse than far-fetched: it is appalling. As a consequence of technological advance in the last few decades, there is practically speaking no limit of a technical character which can be set upon the expansion of government services of all kinds, and hence upon the extension of the power of government over our lives.

For example, the increase in medical knowledge, with the consequent development of new drugs and new diagnostic and surgical techniques, unthought of even a generation ago, means that it is theoretically possible to spend the whole of the national income upon the health services with no other result than to prolong the span of human life by some small margin. Again it would be possible to treble or quadruple government expenditure on roads or housing, and still leave us with an inadequate road system and inadequate housing. And since, in all these fields, the possibilities of advance are generally known—since the motorist knows that there is no technical obstacle to stand in the way of a road system which would allow him to go from one end of this island to the other at an average speed of one hundred and fifty miles per hour, and the valetudinarian knows, even in conditions as they are, that there are resources enough, if only they are properly used, to prolong the wretchedness of his life for two or five or ten years—the pressures against economy and towards expenditure, the predisposition towards inflation in short, becomes irresistible.

An advancing technology makes it possible theoretically to satisfy all these and many other demands, but the attempt to do so can only lead to mounting expenditure and taxation, an ever-increasing degree of state control and the disintegration of the fabric of a free society. This, of course, is something that the politician recognises in a superficial kind of way, and he resolves the problem by the magic word 'priorities'. It is only a matter, we are told, of 'getting our priorities right', which means nothing more than that we give way where the political pressures are strongest. And as these can be switched from one field to another at the drop of a hat, or a march on Trafalgar Square, the magic of priorities is not very powerful. It is essential, nevertheless, for the Conservative party, if a Conservative government is to have any effective influence on events, to clear its mind on these immensely difficult matters. There is little enough sign that it has even begun to do so.*

But Mr. Richard Crossman knows exactly where he is going and where, unless we exert ourselves, he will take us, too. He expresses graphically enough his own view of what will and what ought to happen, in a passage expounding the principle that, in modern conditions, 'the service creates the demand'. He quotes as example 'the technological revolution *which requires us* to spend hundreds of millions of pounds in breaking the sound barrier in order that London passengers can arrive in New York a few hours earlier. And the moment the Concorde is there the demand is created for travelling supersonic. The demand comes second. Science creates it just as faithfully as it creates the demand for kidney machines.'†

---

* There is little that I have been able to find in the party literature, or in the speeches of party leaders, which is not a variation of the song 'Anything you can do I can do better'. This is almost certainly true, but it is not enough. See, for example, the Conservative Central Office Pamphlet *Make Life Better*, p. 16, 'Contrast the Conservative record ... social service spending doubled'; or p. 11, 'We will sort out the structure of ministries and reduce their number.... We will establish a Small Businesses Development Bureau.' Or p. 12, 'Any large business plans its operations. So must the Government if the taxpayer is to get proper value for his money. And these plans should be co-ordinated with the forecasts of private industry.' Who will co-ordinate them? Another kind of Department of Economic Affairs.

† Crossman, op. cit., pp. 9–10 (my italics).

Mr. Crossman foresees a world in which man becomes, quite literally, the slave of his own artefacts. And he may be right. Unless we recover control of our own destiny, he will be proved right. And his solution, too, will come to pass. It is this: '. . . the scientific spirit . . . *forces us out of privacy and private enterprise into ever more complex and ever more universal forms of community activity*. But if the process of expansion cannot be halted it must be planned with a far more articulate scale of priorities and far more sophisticated methods of comparative costing than we at present possess.'*

What does Mr. Crossman see, I wonder, other than a race of pygmies guided and directed by platonic guardians, gigantic, talkative, bespectacled and bland, leading us inexorably to our doom. And what does Mr. Heath see? What is his way of escape from the dilemma on which we are impaled?

Ours after all, is not the first Welfare State in history. Here is an account of another: 'The people were nourished and well-cared for, and they multiplied exceedingly. In the wildest and most inaccessible valleys, in the lofty punas surrounded by snowy heights, in the densest forests, and in the sand clad valleys of the coast, the eye of the central power was ever upon them, and the never failing brain, beneficent though inexorable, provided for all their wants, carried in their tribute, and selected their children for the various occupations required by the state, acording to their several aptitudes.'†

We might do worse, at this juncture in our history, to reflect upon this, the most perfect example of which

* Crossman, op. cit., pp. 9–10 (my italics).
† Sir Clement R. Markham, *The Incas of Peru*, p. 168.

history affords a record, of the socialist, egalitarian, wel-
fare-based state, comprehensive schools (or their equivalent) and all. And we would do well to consider its end,
how Pizarro with a handful of conquistadors, and only a
little bad faith, brought the whole majestic edifice crash-
ing to the ground in a few short months.

EPILOGUE

At the beginning of this essay I said that any political party, to be effective, must have some kind of intellectual and philosophic background to which policy can be referred and which can be communicated to a mass electorate. In the course of it, I have argued that over the whole field of political action, abroad as well as at home, this background of thought and conviction, which alone can influence events, has been lacking in the Conservative party. There has been a failure of leadership.

Of course, the very idea of leadership is suspect in these days, when we have seen with our own eyes what happens to peoples who put themselves in the hands of an inspired leader; but this, in any case, is not in the British tradition. What has been wrong with the leaders of the Conservative party since the war has not been lack of inspiration, but an inability to see things as they are, and to act upon what they see. They have only repeated the shibboleths of the hour, condemning what it is fashionable to condemn and praising what it is fashionable to praise. They have accepted, almost without question, the idea of the omnicompetent state, and that it is within the power of government to meet what is called, in the cant of the day, 'the revolution of rising expectations'. In particular they have been obsessed with the fiction of the middle ground, where issues of the greatest moment are thought to be decided by a minority which cannot be identified, whose very existence is doubtful, but which is supposed to hold the balance of power and to be progressive and forward looking in its outlook.

No political party, it is true, can depart too far from the intellectual orthodoxies of the day without condemning itself to sterility. We can see examples of this in the recent history of the United States. It happened to the Republican party with Mr. Barry Goldwater, and to the Democrats, more than half a century earlier, with William Jennings Bryan. Bryan may have been right when he said that humanity was being crucified on a cross of gold; but even so, it did not save him and his party from a prolonged journey through the political wilderness. But the charge that can be levelled against the Conservatives today is not so much that they accepted the prevailing orthodoxies without question— although this is certainly true—as that they did nothing themselves to influence them. They did nothing to form the climate of opinion: they learned only how to live with it. It is fair to say of the Conservative party that it has never been over-articulate in the expression of its faith, but equally it has never, until now, been so bound a captive to the intellectual arguments of its opponents.

That faith and conviction have a more important place in politics than the modern Conservative is ready to admit does not mean, however, that there is nothing else to be brought into the reckoning, or that considerations of quite a different order, the determination of the ordinary man, for example, to have his share of the good things which are made available by a developing technology, are to be brushed aside as of no account. These are enormously important, but they are not by themselves overwhelmingly decisive.

For the Englishman is less interested in equality than in fairness, and he is too sensible to equate these two very different concepts. Indeed he is far more sensible than most people, at any rate most politicians, suppose. If you talk nonsense to him he seems to drink it down in great gulps, but in his heart he knows that it is nonsense. He will take something for nothing when he can, but he is well aware that he has no right to it; and he has a sneaking contempt for those who tell him that he has—especially if it is a Conservative who tells him. For there is a difference in the voter's attitude towards the two parties. He recognises, even if he does not put it into words, that when the Socialist promises uncovenanted benefits, he is being true to himself, that he is expressing a view of society which he genuinely holds. When a Conservative makes the same offer it appears for what it is—a bribe.

This difference between the two parties is seen most clearly, perhaps, in their attitude towards what is known as the Welfare State. The Socialist genuinely believes that it is wrong, in principle and as a matter of ethics, for the citizen to pay for health or educational services, because if these things are to be paid for their distribution will be unequal. If it were possible so to arrange matters, he would no doubt extend indefinitely the provision of state services without payment, to cover such things as housing, clothing and even food. Only in this way would it be possible to realise in practice the perfect equality which is his ideal.

The Conservative, on the other hand, and on grounds quite other than the practical impossibility of realising it and the acute economic problems which arise from the attempt to do so, sees a society of this kind as something positively degrading in itself. Its members, in his view, are not to be regarded as mature human beings, able to shoulder responsibility and with a capacity for self-development, but rather as eternal children, for whom the necessities of life are provided by an indulgent parent while they themselves are left with a little pocket money to spend on such gewgaws as washing machines, television sets, betting shops or pop records. And yet the Conservative until now, at any rate, has vied with the Socialist in extolling this all-embracing, all pervasive, all-for-nothing idea of social provision.

Of course it is unreasonable to ask a politician, whose survival depends on popular support, to court unpopularity. There is a distinction, however, between that popularity which of its nature is ephemeral, and the kind of support which endures and which has proved, in practice, to be the only solid base for political action. The politician who, throughout his career, expresses a sturdy consistency and independence of outlook has an influence greater by far than that of his more supple colleague doubled up in his effort to keep his ear to the ground, whose only concern is to catch and reflect the fashions of the day.

These are distinctions which the Labour party has recognised as Conservatives have not. Until the days of Mr. Harold Wilson's administration, at any rate, the Labour party, in office or opposition, in fair weather or foul, proclaimed its faith and never deviated from it, regardless alike of facts or electoral consequences. It is true, no doubt, that it has never been backward in attracting votes by the expenditure of public money, but this has

156

been as much to give effect to policies which it has consistently proclaimed, and which can only be realised by
massive public expenditure, as to buy support for them.
It can fairly be said that the Labour party has sought
rather to create trends than to conform to them. In terms
of electoral advantage this may have proved unprofit-
able, for it has meant, and perhaps it always does mean,
that a party so inspired has to spend a great part of its
time in the wilderness. But it has meant also that the
philosophy, the outlook of the Labour party has pre-
vailed even when a Conservative government has been
in office. Those who set the trend, not those who reflect
it, have the real power, on whichever side of the House
of Commons they may be sitting. A Conservative Cabinet will always be a Shadow Cabinet, unless its members
have the capacity, which they have lacked in recent
years, to withdraw from the immediacies of the moment
to refresh themselves at the springs of their faith.

And a part of that faith, and not the most inconsider-
able part of it, is confidence in the good sense and in-
herited experience of the electorate, and in their ability
to distinguish, as the old saw has it, chalk from cheese.
An appeal to the instinctive judgement of the British
people and to their tribal gods—their love of their country, their respect for themselves and for each other (a
respect which has little regard for barriers of class or
creed), their independence and their determination 'not
to be put upon'—will generally be heeded. There will
be times, no doubt, when, whether from that curious insensitivity which a prolonged spell of office seems to
build up in Ministers, or from sheer boredom on the
part of the electorate, or for whatever reason, the pendu-

157

lum will swing the other way. If it were not so, indeed, there would be an end to parliamentary government, of which the essence is a continuing alternation between action and reaction, between consolidation and reform. This opposition is not, as the progressive sees it, an obstacle to advance. It is the condition of advance, and without it there would be none, only a loosening of the bonds of society and a steady slide downhill to anarchy and nihilism.

When all is said, the Conservative party has nothing to lose by basing its appeal on the good sense of the electorate. If the British people have suddenly changed their character, if indeed they are only to be humbugged and bribed, like children with sweetmeats, the game is up—whatever the outcome of the next election, or the one after the next. It is not the future of the Conservative party which is an issue now, or its claim to office. It is the future of parliamentary government, and of society itself.

INDEX